# Riding On A Ponkey

**Rob Goyette**

RIDING ON A PONKEY

Living Waters World Outreach Center
Fernandina Beach, FL

Printed in the United States of America

ISBN: 978-0-578-32073-1

Dedicated to my God, my family and to all those He's so lovingly placed around me, especially my dear wife Christie.

# King Frequents Amelia Island

Our idle talk was suddenly broken with the sound of fishing line singing off of the reel. The hook was set and the fight was on! All of my life I had wanted to catch big game fish like those found here in the waters of Northeast Florida and now it was finally coming true. Well, kind of.... I was not the one actually holding the rod and reel.

You see, I was the first mate on my uncle's charter fishing boat. I had just moved to Amelia Island for the summer to try to figure out my life's purpose.

The fish ran hard before finally breaking the water's surface. The sight of a 120-pound tarpon leaping into the air was almost more than my fresh water upbringing could bear. I can still hear my uncle's advice on how to handle these huge silver fish as they soar into the air. "Tarpon are the king of game fish, Robby. "When they jump you have to bow to them."

*Bow* to them? I remember thinking, "You've got to be kidding!" but he was quite serious. Now I love to fish and I'd have done just about anything to be a part of catching a huge tarpon, but this idea of bowing to the king of fish was a little overboard to me.

My uncle must have seen the reaction in my face as he continued to explain that bowing was a matter of respect for the fish's weight and size. You see, in the water the fish might only weigh 50 pounds. But once he leaps into the air you feel his full weight and power. If you don't bow, the fish is going to break the line, and you're going to lose him.

I've learned a lot since those days, but perhaps the most important thing has been that of bowing to the King. No, not the king of game fish, but the King of Kings, the Lord Jesus Christ. There's no one more worthy of respect and honor than Him. It's been my observation that we all seem to struggle in a common area when it comes to bowing to the King. It seems that just about the time God is getting ready to break onto the scene of our lives, we pull back. Whether it is from fear, insecurity, or perhaps just not knowing what to do, the result is pretty much the same: a lost opportunity to see Him as He is.

Unlike the tarpon, God actually wants to be caught by us. He longs to be near us and to show us His love and power, but we must learn to bow. Not with some outward show of humility, easily counterfeited by our religious activities. Rather with a bow that takes place deep within our hearts that acknowledges Him as King. The motive of this bowing is to know God up close and personal.

Only God knows when and how He will show up next in our lives. Just one word of advice when He does: don't pull back but Bow to the King.

*"O come, let us worship and bow down: let us kneel before the LORD our maker." (Psalm 95:6)*

# Building A Forever House

The day had finally come. With tool pouches on and shovels in hand, my then seven-year-old son and I made our way to the job site. Besides me, no one was more excited than he was. We were getting ready to build our own house and I had promised him he could help.

I must admit the thought of having him by my side and building our family home brought a deep sense of satisfaction. As we made our way through the field and into the woods where our home site was, our fellowship seemed almost heavenly. Father and son, side by side, ready to build a place for their family.

Though his tool pouch, tape measure, and hammer were smaller than mine, his enthusiasm seemed to capture the attention of all the little creatures living in the woods. "Where do we start, dad?" he said.

"Well, first things first," I replied. "Let's look at the blueprints just to be sure things are in order before we start digging."

"Ok," he said, in a tone like that of a professional construction worker. And so we did.

After confirming the layout and a few basic instructions, the digging began, he on one side of the house and me on the other. Anyone who's ever dug a foundation in Florida knows that between sand gnats and tree roots there's just a lot of hard work. Although my son was not complaining, I was curious to how long he was going to last.

Shovel full after shovel full we worked as his obvious zeal and enthusiasm began to wane. It was then, after a period of quiet working, that he broke the silence with words I will never forget. "Dad?" he asked. "Can't we just buy a house?"

I broke into laughter as I realized that he had finally reached his limit. Though his initial excitement had carried him thus far, it was only a matter of time, and I knew it, before he would realize how big the job really was. While that was many years ago, I often remember the experience as I see new believers heading toward the job site with their heavenly Father. Equipped with the same kind of tools and full of godly zeal, it's only a matter of time before each one of us realize that if this house is going to be finished, it will be because of our Father's commitment, not ours.

Please don't misunderstand me. God's heart is bursting with joy to have us at His side building the kingdom. Yet if we think that we, in and of ourselves, have what it takes to finish the work that He's begun, we're sorely deceived. Psalms 127:1 makes it pretty plain: "Except the LORD build the house, they labor in vain that build it: except the LORD keep the city, the watchman wakes but in vain."

Isn't it good to know that though at times we want to quit, God is not angry with us? As a matter of fact, He may even be chuckling. No, not because He's insensitive to the way we're feeling, but rather because He knows our limitations and loves us just the same. As we each find our place laboring at His side, it's my prayer that we'll all slow down for a moment and remember who it is we're working with; the Author and Finisher of our faith.

*"Looking unto Jesus the author and finisher of our faith; who for the joy that was set before him endured the cross, despising the shame, and is set down at the right hand of the throne of God." Hebrews 12:2*

# Riding On A Ponkey

I had just thrown one leg over the small half-pony half-donkey's back when it bolted with everything it had. The crowd of onlookers were amazed as I held on with all my might. I had ridden many things in my life but never something so energetic and determined to throw me off. And that it did -- right into the nearby pond! That's right…into the pond! As I emerged, the youth group which I was then pastoring was in hysterics as I tried to recover my position as their leader.

We had been on a one-day outing at a friend's house, who owned the ornery little creature, when I had been challenged to ride it. The only people that had ridden it before were small children accompanied by an adult walking alongside. I was the first man to sit on its back and impose my will over its life.

As I walked back toward the still laughing crowd, the Ponkey, as I have chosen to call it, stood afar off with what I'm sure was a smile on its face. How do you recover from such an incident? The only thing that made any sense was to swallow my pride and join the crowd in their laughter. The humorous memory still makes me chuckle as I consider the determination the Ponkey had to not be controlled by another.

When we consider Jesus' final entry into the city of Jerusalem, we often remember the worshiping crowd crying their Hosannas to the Son of David. Unfortunately, we often overlook the real worshipper upon which Jesus was riding. You may not agree, but the small colt on which Jesus rode that day was the model of true worship. Let me explain.

Mark's Gospel 11:2 tells about a little colt upon whom no man had ever sat. It was this very colt that Jesus chose to ride upon into Jerusalem. The triumphant entry is about God's victory over all the illegitimate rulers of the earth and that very easily can mean us. The little colt was a shining example of a will surrendered to the only King worthy to rule our lives.

We all despise the idea of someone riding us for their own gain, but it's not so with Jesus. He came not in some flashy, domineering way, but "meek and lowly of heart" riding upon a colt that had no desire to throw Him off. He came to save us not to enslave us, and those who know it are glad to let Him ride.

I suppose the day the Ponkey threw me in the pond I deserved it. He must have known that my motive for riding him was questionable and that I probably didn't have his best interest at heart. It's my prayer that Jesus will find willing vessels doing more than just waiving palm branches. Let's be providing lives on which He might ride into our community.

*"Rejoice greatly, O daughter of Zion; shout, O daughter of Jerusalem: behold, thy king cometh unto thee; He is just, and having salvation; lowly, and riding upon an ass, even upon a colt the foal of an ass." Zech 9:9*

# Evil Into Good

There at the curbside was a lone package, no doubt left behind by one of the many travelers that day. The small, private cab service that used the location for its pick-up site eased into the spot having just completed another successful journey. Or so it seemed. The lone package caught the driver's eye. It presumably belonged to his most recent passenger. If he hurried perhaps he could catch up with him and return his missing goods.

The car door opened and the faithful driver reached for the parcel that would forever change his life. Little did he know the package was a bomb ready to explode as soon as he picked it up. Pindongo lost both his arms that day and the better part of one of his legs.

We were in Indonesia visiting a refugee village where thousands of Christians had fled because of religious persecution. As we stood outside his home, visiting with his wife and children, Pindongo came hobbling down the street with the aid of a faithful friend. It had been almost a year since the tragic incident had forever changed the life of this struggling family.

With tears of gratitude streaming down his face, Pindongo blessed our team in a way I will never forget. "I have nothing of this earth that I can give you," he said. "All I have to offer you are my prayers." Then, out of his brokenness flowed a prayer that would change me forever. There was no anger or unforgiveness toward those who had maimed him but only love and grace.

Pindongo was one of many people we visited who had suffered at the hands of those bent on destroying the testimony of Jesus Christ in the earth. Little did they know that their evil plots would be used to reveal the love and forgiveness of Christ through the very people they were trying to kill. How can someone who has suffered such wrong have so much love and grace in their heart? I'll tell you how -- by the presence of Jesus Christ.

When we consider the sufferings of Christ, may we also be reminded of the power of His resurrection. The Bible is full of examples of God permitting in His wisdom what He can prevent with His power. Such is the case with the crucifixion. The devil would have never carried out his evil plan had he known how God was going to turn it around. Who would have thought that such a horrible event as the crucifixion could be turned into the forgiveness of our sins and the resurrection of the dead?

It's amazing how God has the ability to turn tragedies into blessings and apparent defeat into absolute victory. Evil will never triumph over good. It may boast for a season, but little does it know that in the end it will surrender in full submission to Him who was raised from the dead.

As our world seems to be spinning more and more out of control, it only gives us added reason to celebrate the resurrection. No matter how hard wickedness tries to prevail, it simply serves as the backdrop for the revealing of Jesus Christ.

Though we've not seen Pindongo for several years, and Indonesia seems a world away; his heartfelt prayer still burns within me. Death has been swallowed up by life and evil will always be the servant of good.

*"but we speak God's wisdom in a mystery, even the wisdom that hath been hidden, which God foreordained before the worlds unto our glory: which none of the rulers of this world hath known: for had they known it, they would not have crucified the Lord of glory: " (1 Cor 2:7-8)*

# Learning to Hear The Sound of Truth

The cage door opened and my friend entered. His only weapon was a straightened coat hanger with a small bend in the end. The inhabitants were in absolute chaos as he moved very carefully toward his target.

As I watched from without, not quite sure what to make of the whole thing, I wondered how he would accomplish his goal. Then without warning, he lunged forward and hooked the leg of chicken number one. With feathers flying and the rest of the coop in an uproar, he made his way to the door and placed the chicken in a small cage for transport.

I was getting ready to be the proud owner of four chickens. Though it was not one of my lifelong ambitions, my friend's persistent offer and the thought of fresh eggs was enough to make me willing to try. As we loaded the birds into the back of his truck, I had noticed that one of them was much larger than the rest. "That's a Dominick Chicken," my friend said. "She's not even full grown yet, but when she is, she's going to lay huge eggs." Well Praise God, I remember thinking, if you're going to have chickens, they might as well lay huge eggs!

The truck pulled into my yard and we placed the chickens into the comparatively primitive coop that I had built just for the occasion. Friends and neighbors were somewhat quizzical to my new venture, but in time, I knew they would understand, especially when they saw the huge eggs laid by my Dominick chicken.

A few days later while feeding my new brood, a friend from Mexico dropped by. His name was Chico and he was one of those guys who know a little bit about everything... except chickens, it would seem.

"Hola Roberto!" he said through his heavy Latin accent. "I see you've got some chickens and a rooster."

"Just some chickens," I replied. "That big one is a Dominick chicken and she is going to lay some huge eggs."

"No," Chico said as he paused and slowly shook his head, "that's a rooster." Back and forth we went until finally I realized that our debate was going nowhere. In just a few short days, the arrival of huge eggs would settle the matter.

Well, I was right, at least in part. In a few days the issue was all cleared up. There while peacefully sleeping, I was awakened by the sound of truth. "Cock-a-doodle-doo!" it said. I sat up in my bed and had to confess, "It's a rooster!"

One thing I've learned about truth is that it is what it is. Just because I believe something different doesn't mean the truth is going to change. Such is the case when it comes to the Bible. It is what it is -- the Word of God. We either believe it or we prove it.

As far as I can tell, the primary job of Christians is not to argue about the truth, which only seems to divide us, but to demonstrate it through the way we live our lives. Truth is more than a bunch of theological concepts. In the Gospel of John 14:6 the Bible declares that Truth is a *person* and His name is Jesus. He's the answer to all of our questions. When He is revealed in and through our lives, all the debates that divide us seem to fade away.

My experience raising chickens - and one rooster - came and went many years ago, but the lesson I learned lives on. It's my prayer that God would give us all a love for the sound of truth.

*"Jesus saith unto him, I am the way, the truth, and the life: no man cometh unto the Father, but by me." John 14:6*

# Stabbed In The Dark

It was the first time I had ever agreed to take our youngest daughter flounder gigging. For those of you who don't know what that is, it's the somewhat barbaric act of stabbing a fish as it lies in the sand. Sarah has always been a little adventurous but, to be honest, I wasn't sure how she was going to handle spearing an innocent fish. It was not long after we stepped into the water that my curiosity would be satisfied.

Flounder gigging is something you do at night. For Sarah, the possibility of unknown sea creatures sneaking up on us was enough to keep her clinging tightly to my arm. With a light in one hand, gig in the other, and a car battery floating in an inner tube tied to my belt, the added weight of my daughter pulling on my arm was sure to make for an interesting evening.

It wasn't long after we entered the water that I spotted our first fish. After quickly pointing it out, I instructed her to go ahead and spear him, but she froze and couldn't do it. "You do it!" she said, not quite ready to leave her feminine nature behind. I continued to encourage her knowing that she might not get another chance.

Suddenly, with her eyes closed, she made what appeared to be her best attempt but missed the fish altogether. Though I was sorry to see such a nice fish swim away, I quickly encouraged her and told her that the next fish we would gig together; and that we did. It wasn't long before she was spearing her own fish. Truth be known, she gigged more fish that night than I did. Her confidence had risen to a whole new level. Though she still remained close to my side because of all the unknowns, her fears had all but vanished before the night was over.

I've learned that the Lord doesn't waste a thing, even the somewhat unusual pastime of flounder gigging. He took full advantage of this arm clinging quality time between my daughter and me. It seemed that night that every word that came out of my mouth the Lord turned around and directed it back to me.

Though I was confident and experienced in the sport of flounder gigging, I sure could relate to her feelings of stepping into unknown and uncharted waters. I know just what it is to miss the target all together, though I've done it with eyes wide open. I know what it's like to be encouraged and not condemned in the midst of my failures. I've learned what it means to grow in confidence without ever leaving the side of the One who holds the light. The analogies run on and on but time and space will not allow.

As for me, I received an unexpected double blessing that night. Not only did I have a wonderful memory-making experience with my daughter, but I received fresh encouragement from the Lord. As is usually the case right after God shows me something, I'm required to walk in what I've learned. No matter what you may be facing, know that God is for you and has committed Himself to helping you hit the mark.

*There is no fear in love: but perfect love casteth out fear..."( 1 John 4:18a)*

# Answering The Call

The elevator came to a sudden stop. The only problem was that it was between floors. Ironically, I had just been examining the escape hatch when the sudden stop occurred. "How does a person even reach it?" I remember thinking. I was about to find out.

After pushing all the normal buttons to no avail, I finally decided to pick up the emergency phone. You know the one that as a kid you're told never to touch? If you're like me and have always wondered who's on the other end of such a phone, I'm sorry to report that I don't know. That's right, the phone was dead! What made the matter worse was that I was alone. To my knowledge, I was the only person in the entire building that day.

I was at a retreat site that I frequent for prayer and study and had just gone downstairs to get some ice before settling in. If I had known things would end up like this, I would have just stayed home. In the midst of some prayers, resembling someone talking to himself, and a few yells for help, I discovered a small alarm button on the wall. I pressed it over and over again in hopes that somebody, anybody, might hear and come to my rescue. And that they did.

In a time when I thought that I was all alone, God in His mercy had left a cleaning lady in the building. She was quick to assure me that everything would be all right and got a hold of the maintenance man who finally got me out.

After settling back into my room with a bucket of slightly melted ice, I was finally ready to get on with the important business of prayer and study. Then it happened: with laptop computer comfortably positioned on my lap, Bible opened and worship music playing, I heard the unmistakable sound of the elevator alarm. I couldn't believe it. Someone else was stuck.

I have to be honest: my initial response was not very Christ-like. Didn't they know I had come here not to be disturbed? I waited for a few moments in hopes that someone else would answer the call but it didn't happen.

All fingers were pointing at me as the Holy Spirit reminded me of where I had just come from. It never ceases to amaze me how soon we forget all that God has done for us in our time of need. I quickly put all my religious activities aside and returned to the place where I had just been rescued.

Be assured that no one had to tell me what to say. I had learned it first-hand from the cleaning woman, "It's going to be all right. I know someone who can get you out of there."

The message has great spiritual application. This is the very reason that Jesus came into the world, not to condemn us but to rescue us. He was the only one not trapped by sin and, therefore, the only one qualified to get us out.

I know that God saw my heart that day when I had genuinely pulled aside just to be with Him. In His loving way He had once again reached down to rescue me. This time not just from being stuck on an elevator, but more importantly from the subtle trap of any religious activity that is void of the love of Christ.

May the Lord remind us all where we've come from and give us hearts to respond to those in need.

*"If a man says, I love God, and hateth his brother, he is a liar: for he that loveth not his brother whom he hath seen, cannot love God whom he hath not seen. And this commandment have we from Him, that he who loveth God love his brother also." 1 John 4:20-21*

# Paper Mill Provides Solution

There I was standing shin deep in a roadway full of thousands of gallons of mushy paper pulp. My new expensive leather boots were soaking wet.

We all stood in amazement as the huge holding tanks spilled over into the streets. "Your job is to clean it up," we were told. "Don't worry about the tanks running over; we'll take care of that."

With large push brooms in hand, we began what seemed to be the impossible task. As new employees, we couldn't help but wonder if this was going to be our job every day and we were so glad to find out that it was not. We all spread out and went to work pushing the heavy oatmeal-like paper pulp toward the nearby drains. Hour after hour we worked, each doing our best to put more in the drain than the tanks might occasionally spill out.

Those in charge were good to their word and fixed the overflow problem. Our job, however, had just begun. At our current rate of progress, it seemed we would be there for days pushing the elusive pulp as it ran around the edges of our brooms.

I don't remember whose idea it was, but I will never forget the results. As we were spread out in our various areas, each working hard to get the job done, someone suggested we try working together instead of alone. Initially not everyone bought into the idea but it didn't take long for them to catch on.

It seemed that while working alone each push of the broom lost as much around the edges as it was able to moved forward. However, when we came together an amazing thing happened. By joining the edges of our brooms, we were able to form a large C shape that allowed us to capture much of what we had been losing while working alone. As we all pushed, the results were truly astounding. What seemed like it would take days to complete was knocked out in just a few short hours.

Though our feet were wet and we were tired, large grins filled our faces while we experienced the reward of working together. Even the bosses were impressed with how a group of perfect strangers could pull together and accomplish so much in such little time.

If there's ever been a time to remove the barriers that keep us from locking our brooms together it's now. It's quite plain that the job of spreading the Good News is much bigger than any one person can handle. Though at times it may seem that the more we push the more spills out of life's tank, it's quite plain that God is still in control. Our job is not to figure out how our Boss is going to fix all of life's problems, but rather to examine ourselves and figure out how we're going to get our assignment done.

Whether we're talking about our families, our churches, or even our civil government for that matter, the principle remains the same. We need each other. Sometimes I have to wonder if God doesn't just let the streets fill up to see if we are going to work together to get the job done.

*"Two are better than one because they have a good reward for their labor." Ecclesiastes 4:9*

# God's Provision Is In His Word

Everything in me wanted to run. The pressures of life had knocked me off balance and left me in a state of confusion and uncertainty. As I sat on the worn-out couch, which represented my overall decor, I pondered all my soon coming bills.

I was a young man of only 20 years old and just starting out in life. The house I was renting, quaint as it was, was old and in need of lots of repair. All of my teenage illusions of independent living were quickly fading away. My temporary job had just ended and although engaged in a careful search for adequate employment, nothing even close to what I needed seemed anywhere in sight.

"I've got to do something," I remember thinking, although I was already doing everything I knew to. The idea of just waiting was more than I could bear. As I got up and made my way to the door, I felt the Lord tug on my heart and tell me to sit down. Though at first I resisted, I knew that my anxious attitude was sure to get me nowhere. "Ok God, what do You want?"

After a few moments of quieting my soul, it became clear that I needed to spend some time reading God's Word. There on a small wooden shelf across the room lay an old worn-out Bible I had retired months earlier because it was falling apart. I had to be careful not to drop its loose pages as I sat down to offer my best attempt at listening to a God who seemed so far away.

What took place next was more than I could conceive. As I randomly opened the Bible, I couldn't believe my eyes. There looking me right in the face was a $100 bill! After a moment of absolute shock, I did what every one of you would have done. I grabbed the Bible by its binding, hung its pages face down, and began to shake it to see if there was anything else in there.

I later learned that my dad had placed it there months before in an anonymous attempt to bless me in those somewhat sparse years. He had assumed that I would be using that Bible on a daily basis and would find the provision in a timely manner. Timely manner it was; just not mine or his, but God's.

Though the $100 bill did not cover all my expenses, it provided more than enough faith and encouragement to carry me through that very important season of my life. Just think about it: the whole time I was overwhelmed and anxious about tomorrow, God had already made provision. It was sitting right there in my Bible. I just didn't know it.

Jesus made it quite plain when He told us to seek first the Kingdom of God and His righteousness, and in doing so all the other necessities of life would be provided for (Matt.6:33). How is it that the things that ought to be first in our lives are often put last? What joy there is in knowing that the creator of all things is a loving Father who has placed our provision in His Word! Though I've never found more money in my Bible, be assured I read it a whole lot more than I use to.

Why wait for a crisis to happen before we draw near to such a loving and faithful God?

*"This book of the law shall not depart out of thy mouth, but thou shalt meditate thereon day and night, that thou mayest observe to do according to all that is written therein: for then thou shalt make thy way prosperous, and then thou shalt have good success." (Joshua 1:8)*

# The Path of the Just

Single file and in almost perfect formation they walked. Their stride was steady and measured as if being trained by a branch of our armed services. They were on a common path well worn by their daily routine. One by one, they made their way to the place where they were sure to find their provision.

They were Nubian goats heading out to pasture not far from where I was getting ready to build my new house. The sight was nothing unusual, in and of itself, but the path they were on made absolutely no sense.

Just a few weeks prior, my friend and I pulled down the fence that had once forced the goats to walk all the way around to the gate before entering the pasture. Yet there they were, still using the path that was no longer necessary. With heads bobbing up and down and eyes fixed on the trail, their procession was almost comical. Now that the fence was gone, the pasture they were heading for was only a short distance away but the old familiar trail was all they knew.

Everything in me wanted to run out in front of them and say, "Hey, what are you doing? Lift up your heads, the fence is gone!" but I knew they wouldn't get it. I could almost imagine them saying, "This is the way we've always done it, now leave us alone, you're slowing us down."

Though I hate to admit it, experience tells me that we're not much different. We tend to be creatures of habit and once we've found something that seems to work, it's hard to get us to change. True, there's nothing wrong with holding on to things that are serving us well, but it sure is a shame when those very things keep us from seeing something better.

How is it that which is good can become the enemy of what is best? God's heart must ache every time He sees us taking the long way around. Maybe it's just me, but I'm almost certain there have been times when angels are jumping up and down in front of me trying to get my attention. They're probably saying, "Hey you! What are you doing? Lift up your head, the fence is gone!"

The Bible says in Ephesians 2:13-14 that we who were once far away are now made near by the blood of Jesus. The text further states that He, Jesus, has removed the wall that once kept us back from the promises and blessings of God.

Why is it then that we keep taking the long way around, always feeling like knowing God has to be some difficult task attached to our works? Though our disciplines and good conduct play an important role in life, they are never to be confused with the path that leads to God.

I'm convinced that knowing God ought to be the greatest joy of our lives. When we think about Him, it should not be with thoughts of work and duty, but rather of joy and desire.

If you're like me, at times feeling your head bobbing up and down following the familiar path, maybe it's time to look up. The fence is gone and immediate access is available to all who are willing to change their course and believe.

*"Come unto me, all ye that labor and are heavy laden, and I will give you rest. Take my yoke upon you, and learn of me; for I am meek and lowly in heart: and ye shall find rest unto your souls. For my yoke is easy, and my burden is light." (Matthew 11:28-30)*

# Time Out for Eternal Things
## (Big Bertha)

Ten, nine, eight, seven, six, five.... the countdown had begun. The huge rocket sat perched on its launch pad as if starring into outer space. An excitement filled the air as all the spectators watched in anticipation of what would happen next. The question as to whether it would even fly seemed painted on everyone's faces.

I was among the crowd that day and rightly so. You see I had built the Big Bertha rocket; the only one, I might add, in my entire sixth-grade class. For whatever the reason, all the other students had chosen to build smaller, more conservative rockets but I was drawn to Big Bertha.

Three, two, one, lift off! With only a slight hesitation, it shot into the air. I was so proud of my accomplishment, when suddenly something went terribly wrong. What began as a perfect ascent turned into a downward dive. Still under the full power of its engine, the rocket had changed course and was now heading right at my sixth-grade class.

Like soldiers running from an incoming bomb, we all scattered in an attempt to save our lives. I wish I could give you more details but it's hard to watch and run at the same time. Thankfully, the only injury that day was to my pride. What had gone wrong?

After a careful examination of the rocket's remains, the problem became quite clear. One of the steering fins at the base of the rocket was not straight. In the hurried, once -a-week classroom setting given for construction, I had not taken the necessary time to align the fins properly. Looking back, I was more focused on my rocket's powerful engine and the fact that it stood taller than everyone else's. Little did I know that my wrong focus, coupled with limited class time, would cost me so much.

I can't help but consider the parallel that exists when we gather for our relatively brief Sunday morning church services. Often hurried by all the important stuff waiting outside, we quickly process eternal things in hopes that everything will fly right on the day of launch. It's very plain to me that in order to be successful in life, we need to slow down and take full advantage of every opportunity God has given us to get things right.

Whether we're preachers or homemakers, members of big churches or small, it really doesn't matter. God wants us all to be successful and that success requires more than a hurried session on Sunday mornings.

Experience has taught me when we work on things in little spurts and with limited time invested, we always run the risk of failure. Such was the case with my Big Bertha rocket. Outwardly impressive, but unable to reach the heights for which it was created.

True success is not measured by size or power, but quality and integrity. So much of what impresses us here on earth won't even get off the launch pad when it comes to eternal things. My prayer is that the fruit of our lives will not scatter people, but rather draw them to Jesus.

*"therefore thus saith the Lord Jehovah, Behold, I lay in Zion for a foundation a stone, a tried stone, a precious corner-stone of sure foundation: he that believeth shall not be in haste." (Isaiah 28:16)*

# More than Idle Talk

There it was: an early model souped-up racecar with large slick tires and hood scoop coming right down the road toward my buddies and me. We were all around 17 years old and just hanging out together at a local park in Burlington, Vermont. The car, though outwardly in mint condition, sounded terrible as it sputtered and spit while observing the speed limit of our little lakeside gathering place.

What a shame, it seemed, to have such a nice looking car that ran so rough. You would have thought that anyone willing to spend so much money making the outside look good would have done at least the same for what was under the hood.

Then it happened. Unexpectedly to us all, but not to its driver, the car suddenly came alive with a sound I will never forget. In all my life, I'd never heard an engine that sounded so good, so in tune and so powerful. We were shocked at its apparent change in nature. As it sped away it didn't take us long to figure it out. That car was not designed to idle, it was built to run.

I've often thought back to that day when I find myself spitting and sputtering through life, outwardly looking ok but on the inside knowing there's something so much more.

The bottom line is this: people just don't idle well. We weren't designed to. Just because we spit and sputter, it's no indicator of who we really are. When we read the Scriptures we find out the potential that God has put under the hood of each believer.

The Bible tells us in the book of Romans 8:29 that Jesus is the "first-born of many brethren." In essence He's the first one off the assembly line. The perfect man and prototype of all that God ever intended us to be like. Not only did He do things like walk on water and raise the dead, so did His disciples. He healed broken hearts and restored lost souls and so did His disciples. He refused to idle through life in front of a lost and dying world and so did His disciples.

While I've never physically raised the dead or walked on water, neither am I suggesting that's the evidence of being in right relationship with God. Aren't you glad? I have, however, come to a couple of basic conclusions about God's ultimate purpose for each of our lives.

The first is that we've all been created in God's own image and likeness. Though sin, for a season, has robbed us of our inheritance, God has purchased us back by the blood of His son Jesus. He has in His resurrection waived His "paid in full" receipt for all to see.

Secondly, while none of us is perfect, His grace is sufficient for us. It is working in us until we are completely restored in spirit, soul, and eventually even in body. I find great encouragement by these simple truths. Though I may sputter along at times, I'm not defined by my current experience but rather by the perfect image, which Jesus came to reveal and restore. How wonderful it is to lift the hood and see what great potential God has placed on the inside of every believer!

Though this natural world boasts of all its speed limit signs, our hope is not natural but supernatural and lies in Christ who is sure to finish the work He has begun.

*"For whom he foreknew, he also foreordained to be conformed to the image of his Son, that he might be the firstborn among many brethren: and whom he foreordained, them he also called: and whom he called, them he also justified: and whom he justified, them he also glorified. (Romans 8:29-30)*

# Worship Helps Us See

Dirt was flying everywhere! Around the corner and up the hill they came; one after the other they sailed into the air, each one pushing the limits of man and machine.

As I hung over the fence, captured by the sight and sound of some of the world's best riders, my mind drifted and dreamed about the day I would be among their ranks. Bike after bike, lap after lap, I studied their individual style and techniques, as the best riders widened their lead from the rest of the pack.

As far back as I can remember I had always wanted to race professional Motocross. For those of you not sure what that is, it's the rather dangerous, yet very exciting sport of racing motorcycles on a rugged dirt track. Now I know that seems a far cry from being a pastor, and living the Christian life, but you'd be amazed at the similarities.

In the race that day, much like the race of life, at any given moment you could find a huge variety of skill and personal predicament. Some riders found themselves stalled and in a feverish attempt to restart their engines, while others had lost control and were off the track altogether. There were the conservative riders and the not so conservative, the cautious and the crazy. Some just content to finish the race and others fully set on winning. One thing was for sure, just to be among their ranks would have been a dream come true for the majority of the crowd that day. They made it look so easy, like vendors at the county fair demonstrating how to play and win their games, each rider made you feel like you could do it.

As they sailed through the air, I watched for the first time one of the most amazing aspects of the sport I had ever seen, the use of tear off lenses. One by one while soaring dozens of feet above the crowd, riders would let go with one hand to tear off clear plastic disposable lenses from their goggles. What a concept! As you can imagine, all the mud and dirt flying around really impairs a rider's vision. Not only had they discovered a way to clear it, but they found the perfect time to do it; while in the air.

Now I realize this may seem a far stretch for some of you and the idea of letting go of the handle bars may appear totally reckless, but for me it's a beautiful picture of what our times of worship are supposed to be like. Freed momentarily from the need to hold on to the handlebars, we are able to lift our hearts with our hands and receive new vision. Let's be honest, life is a lot like a motocross race. Complete with mud, bumps and difficult turns, and we all need time to gain a fresh perspective on things.

Our times of personal devotion and corporate worship are perfect opportunities for letting go and being renewed. May God grant us all a fresh appreciation for the wonderful privilege of His presence and the benefit of fresh vision to finish the race.

*"Blessed are the pure in heart: for they shall see God." Matthew 5:8*

# Miracle Oil That Cures

By the thousands they come, not hard to kill, just hard to keep up with. Bite after bite they leave us all wondering what went wrong with God's Creation.

In case you don't know, I'm talking about sand gnats. It's hard to believe that something so small can bite so hard. I've never seen one under a microscope but I'm sure they're all teeth. What a joy it was to learn of the Avon product called Skin So Soft. Just rub it on and the gnats are drowning in its fragrant oil.

As a young man, I spent my first years in Florida working construction. Almost every day you learned to anticipate the droves of undesirable gnats. As a part of our morning routine, not only would we offload tools and set up sawhorses, we would anoint ourselves with fresh oil. As you know, construction workers tend to be fairly rugged individuals and don't see themselves as users of fragrant Avon products. However, without fail, day after day I watched and participated in the ritual anointing that seemed to offer the only real hope. Even the toughest of men would eventually use it if the gnats were bad enough. I remember each daily application bringing a sense of great victory. Sound exaggerated? Not if you've been there.

While on a recent trip to Israel, I was interested to learn that shepherds anoint their sheep with oil for basically the same reason. A special oily mixture is applied that keeps the sheep from the constant torment of insects. It's this very thought that King David picks up on in the 23rd Psalm when he describes the Lord as his shepherd. Having been a shepherd himself, David was well acquainted with the torment that sheep face on a daily basis. With no way of anointing themselves, sheep are totally dependent upon their shepherd. Such was the case with David, though he was King. It's clear he had a host of annoying issues constantly buzzing around his life. In a simple yet profound comparison, he knew that his only hope for relief was in the Good Shepherd.

It seems there's always something distracting us from our mission in life. I've come to believe that the little annoying things that we all face have a great purpose. Somehow, God in His wisdom has left them here to remind us of our need for Him. Only as we stay in close relationship with the Good Shepherd can we receive His special anointing upon our lives. Sure, there are a lot of products out there that claim the ability to release us from life's cares, but none like that which the Lord provides. Over the course of my life, I've tried many things, some good and some not so good. Like the tough construction worker, it took me a long time before I was ready to bow and receive God's provision.

Though I'm no longer building houses but people, my daily routine is pretty much the same. I've learned that before I launch out into my work I must check in with the Lord and get some fresh oil and grace for the day. What a sense of victory still comes over my life every time I bow and receive His provision.

He knows how to keep us free from the little things that have such a big bite.

*"Thou preparest a table before me in the presence of mine enemies: thou anointest my head with oil; my cup runneth over. Surely goodness and mercy shall follow me all the days of my life: and I will dwell in the house of the LORD for ever." (Psalm 23:5-6)*

# Come to the Kingdom

Never before had we visited so many countries in such a short period. Mexico, France, Italy, Norway, Germany, Morocco, China, Japan and now we were in England…. Well, kind of. Truth be known, we were at Disney's Epcot Center and I wasn't feeling that well. I don't know if it was the sitting through the time-share sales pitch, or the inclement weather, but I had a throbbing headache and all this at what was supposed to be a time for rest and relaxation.

As we walked among the English architecture, the sound of a street crier caught our ears. Dressed in Old English clothing and accompanied by a couple of women in the same, a crowd was forming for what looked like some kind of street drama. It was clear that a little laughter might do me good, not to mention the fact that my feet were killing me from walking around the world. After some basic instructions for the crowd, the show began. It didn't take long to figure out, that though this drama was being put on by professionals, it was designed for everyone to be involved.

"King Arthur and the Recovery of the Holy Grail" ought to be interesting I thought, as one of the women held up a crown declared to be that of King Arthur. The only problem was there was no one to play the part. Then suddenly she began to walk through the crowd not far from where I was and a horrible thought went through my mind. "Oh no, she's getting ready to draw some unsuspecting soul into this drama and it might be me!"

Much to my relief, the crown landed on a kingly looking individual standing just a few feet away. Laughter filled the crowd as he resigned to make the best of his new calling. "That was close," I thought, based on the way I was feeling and my somewhat rotten attitude. I sure would not have made a good king.

Then it happened: my greatest fear came upon me. Out into the crowd came the town crier announcing me as one of King Arthur's knights complete with an Old English vest to put on. All eyes were on me including my wife who knew just how I was feeling. Somehow, here laughter seemed louder than all the rest. What's a person to do in such a case? Called and chosen, but not very willing. I wanted to watch the show, but now I was in it.

I suppose that God knew just what I needed that day. Though the laughter was good like a medicine, the change of heart came when I got my eyes off my own needs and answered the call. As a pastor, I've had the privilege of being on both sides of the equation. I know what it is like to be in the crowd, just wanting to watch, and I know what it's like being a recruiter for the greatest story ever told.

One thing is for sure, our deliverance and fulfillment are not found in self-preservation but in surrender to the will and purposes of God. Perhaps you see yourself as just one of the crowd, but be assured God's got other things on His mind. Don't be afraid; He actually knows just what He's doing. Before each of us ever came on the scene, the script was already written and we're in it. May God grant us all the grace to accept our role in the proclaiming of greatest story ever told, the good news of Jesus Christ. Who knows, maybe you've come to kingdom for such a time as this.

*"For if you altogether holdest your peace at this time, then shall there enlargement and deliverance arise to the Jews from another place; but you and your father's house shall be destroyed: and who knoweth whether you art come to the kingdom for such a time as this?" (Esther 4:14)*

# Needing A time of Cleansing

The sound of a slap followed by a series of cowboy like yells gave way to one very frightened calf. I had no idea they could run so fast! My older brother Ricky, now several yards behind, was the instigator of what would prove to be one of my most vivid childhood memories.

I was on the terrified calf now running at full speed through the open barn looking for what I assume was its mother. I don't know whose eyes were wider, the calves or mine, but one thing was for sure, we both wanted to see me get off.

It all began while visiting relatives who owned the large dairy farm in northern Vermont. As the adults sat around the old kitchen table engaged in what I'm sure was meaningful conversation, my brother decided to take me on a tour of the farm where he had spent his last summer. I don't know what it is about big brothers, but they seem to have a special ability when it comes to getting little brothers to do things they ought not. Such was the case with Ricky and me. He had assured me that riding dairy cows was a common practice and that we could ride one together. "All you've got to do is get on," he said. "I'll back the cow out of the stall and jump on with you." *Right!*

I've since forgiven my brother for abandoning me in what was clearly to be a shared experience. With arms tightly around the cow's neck and a pace equal to that of a thoroughbred racehorse, I made one of life's worst decisions. Rather than hold onto the panic-stricken cow, now racing toward the main herd, I decided to jump in an attempt to reach the nearby feeding trough. As fate would have it, I came up just short of my target and landed on a floor covered in about six inches of manure. The tractor had just finished pushing the fresh pile together, no doubt just for the occasion. There I was, covered from head to toe. Though thoroughly embarrassed by my predicament, I was so glad to fall into the hands of a loving family who were able to recognize the real me underneath all the other stuff. Never in my entire life has a shower felt so good.

I see a beautiful picture of the love of Jesus in this somewhat humorous story. Like my parents did for me, Jesus sees right passed all our issues and loves us for who we really are - sons and daughters of the Most High God. He never confuses our issues with our identity. Whether it's to a prostitute or tax collector, religious person or criminal, Jesus' message has always been the same. God loves you and me and sees the real us underneath all the stuff.

How wonderful it is to know that we can come to Him no matter what our condition is! Though it's true the stench of sin separates us from meaningful fellowship with God, He has provided a cleansing stream that washes away all our shame. Why go through life trying to cover up the obvious? We've all fallen and need to return home for a good cleaning up.

The old hymn says it well, "What can wash away our sins? Nothing but the blood of Jesus." Nowhere else will you find a cleansing that feels so good!

*"If we say that we have no sin, we deceive ourselves, and the truth is not in us. If we confess our sins, he is faithful and just to forgive us our sins, and to cleanse us from all unrighteousness." (! John 1:8-9)*

# Finding Things We Already Have

The plane door opened and we stepped out into the balmy night air. It didn't take long to figure out that we were tolerated, but not welcomed guests. Armed guards, with fully automatic weapons, met us as we entered the airport's main terminal in an attempt to claim our bags.

This was the moment we all knew we would face. We were a team of five carrying Bibles and Sunday school supplies to the persecuted church of communist Cuba.

As the baggage conveyor made its rounds, we did our best to smile back at the cold stares that filled the room. Moment after moment we waited, but before long it became clear that seven of our ten bags were missing. They were lost, or worse yet, confiscated. Neither scenario was very encouraging.

It just so happened that the three bags that arrived belonged to my wife and I and had our clothes and a few small items that gave no cause for concern to the communist officials. "Your other bags are lost," said the guard behind the counter, "and it's likely to be several days before we find them." Ok God, what do we do now? Not only had we lost the bulk of our supplies, but the clothing and personal belongings of our teammates were missing as well.

As is always the case, God's ways are not our ways. Little did we know that our lost baggage would provide a vivid taste of what Christians face all over the world in countries where their faith is not welcome. For the next week and a half, our team members were forced to live with only one change of clothes and no Bible - stuff we take for granted here in the U.S.A.

We shared what items we could but the one that made the greatest impact was our Bibles. Did you know that in many places of the world it's not uncommon for Christians to pass around one page of a Bible among hundreds of people? We sure had no reason to be complaining. As you can imagine, our times of preaching and teaching took on a whole new light. The very reason we had come, to bring Bibles to those who have not, we were now having to experience.

Why is it that sometimes we have to lose something before we really appreciate it? Though Cuba has changed some over the years, its close proximity to the United States still stands as a stark reminder of what it's like to live in a country whose government denies God.

The remainder of our bags arrived just prior to our leaving. We were able to pick them up at a special site designated for lost luggage. When we opened them up, not one thing had been disturbed! Not only had God provided a way to get more Bibles into Cuba, but also had visited us with a fresh appreciation for our Bibles that we often take for granted.

Though our country is plagued with many of its own issues, there's no other place like it in the entire world. With multiple Bibles lying around in many of our homes and freedom of speech and press, may we not forget those who have never had the chance to hear the good news.

God forbid that we ever have to lose what we have in order to appreciate it.

*"How sweet are Your words unto my taste! yea, sweeter than honey to my mouth! Through Your precepts I get understanding: therefore I hate every false way. Your word is a lamp unto my feet, and a light unto my path." (Psalm 119:103-105)*

# I Once Was Blind But Now I See

The door swung open to a place we had never been before. Much to our surprise, we had stumbled upon a house having some kind of dinner party. The middle-aged man that answered the door was quite amused by my sister and me, as we stood before him with our eyes tightly closed each holding a small coffee can in our hand.

"Money for the blind," we said, expecting that our closed eyes framed by our little faces would pull on heartstrings and bring in some easy money.

"Hold on one minute," the man at the door said, "I'll be right back."

I don't remember whose idea it was or exactly how old we were, maybe six or seven, but up to this point, our plan seemed to be working quite well. The few houses we'd already visited had been very generous and dropped some coins in our cans adding fuel to our mission. It all began when our parents had gone out for the evening and left all five Goyette children with a babysitter. Though we hadn't wandered far from home, I'm sure we neglected to tell the sitter about our little plan.

As we waited for the man at the door to return, the temptation to open our eyes was almost more than we could bear. Suddenly the sound of several other voices filled our ears. "Quick, come and look," they said, as the house full of guests made their way into the foyer to behold us. Perhaps we were the first blind children some of them had ever seen!

"We had struck it rich," I thought. "Surely with all these people so taken by our cause, our coffee cans would be running over."

Then, out of the midst of the crowd came two very familiar voices: Mom and Dad. Somehow, we had landed at the very dinner party they were attending. Miraculously our once blind eyes could now see. Beginning with a little squint, then a half-slit peek, it only took a few moments for our full sight to be restored. Never before had we been able to see so clearly! It's amazing how God's healing power flows into our lives when we are faced with truth.

My parents, God bless them, had enough wisdom to know that our new eyesight needed a chance to put it to use. So, beginning with the last house we had visited, we set out to give back all the change we had collected. House by house we went explaining how the truth had opened our eyes and we would no longer be needing the money.

Though we don't always appreciate it at the moment, thank God for the truth. It's the very thing the Bible says that makes us free. I have to believe that God was the one ordering our steps that day and, in His mercy, decided not to let us go through life holding out our little coffee cans. I understand we were just children, but deep inside every human being is a longing for something more. Try as we may to fill the void with money and other things, nothing will ultimately satisfy us but a personal relationship with Jesus Christ.

As for me, I'm grateful the Lord loved me enough to tell me the truth. I know quite well what the old hymn means when it says, "Amazing grace how sweet the sound that saved a wretch like me, I once was lost but now I'm found, was blind but now I see."

*"The people which sat in darkness saw great light; and to them which sat in the region and shadow of death light is sprung up. From that time Jesus began to preach, and to say, Repent: for the kingdom of heaven is at hand." (Matthew 4:16-17)*

# Where are the Life Preservers?

The large sport fishing boat dipped deep into the valley of a huge breaking wave. None of us realized how big it really was. The glass and wooden panels protecting the cabin area gave way as dangerous amounts of seawater flooded the bow of the boat.

It was my first full day as a resident of Northeast Florida and I had been looking forward to spending my summer as first mate on my uncle's charter fishing boat. The day had begun with a visit to the city docks, when unexpectedly I was invited to help on a charter heading out to sea. Though I wasn't dressed or prepared for the occasion, my uncle and I figured the experience would do me good. Little did we know that in just a few short moments I would be on a sinking boat.

As we made our way out through the jetties, the four passengers (two couples in their mid to late sixties) were clearly concerned, as was I, by the unusually large waves that day. "Things will get smoother once we get outside the jetties," the captain said, "Just hold on, it won't be much longer."

Those words seemed to lose all their comfort as we stared down into the cabin now filled with water. Unable to see what had happened, the captain was sitting high on his chair busy steering the boat towards the open sea.

It was then that one of the women asked the critical question I had no answer for. "Where are the life preservers?" she said, assuming I would know. I'll never forget the feeling of not having the answer to one of life's most important questions. Not only was I unable to help our passengers, but I didn't even know how to save myself.

The story reminds me of how important it is for believers to be properly equipped for the ministry God has entrusted to them. With world events carrying us all up and down as though riding on the waves of a troubled sea, it's more important than ever for each person who names the name of Christ to understand their role in this troubled world.

In the book of Obadiah, verse 21 the Bible says that "saviors (plural) shall come up on mount Zion." Though it's true that there is only one Savior who died for our sins, Jesus Christ, He has left all true believers with the critical job of pointing others to Him. It's for this very reason that the apostle Paul told Timothy to pay close attention to his calling, because in doing so he would both save himself and those who would hear him. (1Tim.4:14-16)

Though in times of prosperity people seem disinterested, it never ceases to amaze me how things change when the boat starts filling up with water. Whether it's a national crisis, hurricanes sweeping through the Gulf Coast, a death in the family, or marital conflict, God has placed His church right in the middle of it all. Though as believers we've all been called to help on the Lord's fishing boat, the real question still seems to be: where are the life preservers?

*"You are the salt of the earth: but if the salt have lost his savour, wherewith shall it be salted? it is thenceforth good for nothing, but to be cast out, and to be trodden under foot of men. You are the light of the world. A city that is set on an hill cannot be hid. Neither do men light a candle, and put it under a bushel, but on a candlestick; and it giveth light unto all that are in the house. Let your light so shine before men, that they may see your good works, and glorify your Father which is in heaven." (Matthew 5:13-16)*

# Handling Unexpected Guests

First it was one, then another and then another. Almost out of nowhere, our house had become the home of some very unwanted guests. Little black fleas that had no doubt been carried in by our cats.

Did I say *our* cats? Truthfully, they belong to my wife. She is the one who pours all the love and care into them. When they're having problems, they can count on her to rescue them. Though they both are great cats and are quite welcome in our house, the presence of fleas immediately disqualifies them from that privilege.

I must confess that it was my wife who called the bug man and my wife who treated them both for fleas. My main concern was to keep the fleas out. I'm sure that if cats could speak, they would be praising my wife and not me. You see, she was most concerned with doing whatever it took to restore them to the comforts and benefits of our home.

This is so much like the God of the Bible. Though our sins will surely disqualify us from His presence, His primary concern is always that of restoring us to our place. I realize that this illustration seems a little ridiculous, but no more so than the way we tend to treat people who are carrying things we don't want to be around.

The whole time our cats were outside waiting for the go ahead to return, I was the policeman of the family. Every time the door opened and closed, I was there to be sure they did not sneak in prematurely. I'm sure that God places "policemen" in every home, and perhaps every local church, but oh how careful we must be not to miss God's heart.

Like the older brother in the story of the prodigal son found in Luke 15, I've always found it interesting how it's possible to be in our Father's house but not have our Father's heart. Yes, it's true that our sins will separate us from God, but it's also true that He has made a wonderful provision for us in Jesus Christ. Like the prodigal son, if we are willing to acknowledge the error of our ways, God is ever ready to fully restore us to our place.

My wife's willingness to step outside the comforts of our air-conditioned home to comb and treat our cats is a beautiful picture of the heart of God for every human being. Jesus did not come to condemn us but to deliver us from evil and restore us back to our place in God.

The bottom line is this: anytime we become a policeman of righteousness more than a lover of people, we miss the very purpose for which Jesus came. In fact, righteousness and self-righteousness look a lot alike; one simply has the heart of God and the other does not.

It's so good to know, fleas or not, God loves you and me and is committed to getting us back to where we belong. Our part is to come under His loving hand and let Him deliver us from all the unwanted stuff we may be carrying.

*"For God so loved the world, that he gave his only begotten Son, that whosoever believeth in him should not perish, but have everlasting life. For God sent not his Son into the world to condemn the world; but that the world through him might be saved." (John 3:16-17)*

# Finding Hidden Treasure

The front door to the old farmhouse groaned open as Mike offloaded his tools to start the long-awaited renovations. Little did he know that just beneath the surface of the cracking plaster walls was hidden treasure that would more than pay for the entire home. Built in the early 1900's, the house gave no clue to the family secret concealed within its walls. For Mike, it was just a project home in need of lots of repair.

After borrowing the needed money from his aunt and signing the remaining paper work, it was finally his! At last he could begin moving some of those awkwardly placed walls. Never in a thousand years would he have imagined what was about to happen next.

With hammer in hand, and visions of wide-open spaces in mind, Mike began the difficult task of tearing out the old walls. It was then the house had no choice but to give up its secret. As his hammer broke through one of the walls, the sound of breaking glass and falling silver coins filled his ears. There on the floor in front of him lie several hundred silver half dollars from the mid 1940's. The original homeowners had placed them there after the Great Depression, determined to never again be without money. Somehow their secret, stored in glass mason jars, had never been handed off to the next generation and now belonged to someone else.

After recovering from the initial shock, Mike began to pull away more and more of the old plaster that covered the security of a family now long gone. Before it was all over, more than 100 quart-size mason jars were found, worth between $400-600 per quart. How would you like to have a pantry full of those preserves?

I can't help but wonder how those who saved and put all those coins in the wall left without telling someone they were there? Likely, their fear of going without caused them to keep their secret to themselves until they finally died. What a shame. How is it that fear of the unknown and self-preservation rob us of the privilege of blessing and being blessed?

Prov.11:24 says "One man gives freely, yet grows all the richer; another withholds what he should give, and only suffers want." Interestingly enough the very things that we think make us secure are often the very things robbing us of our temporal and eternal rewards.

As for me, I've decided I want to live in the blessings of God and invest in eternal things. I'm not suggesting that having a savings account is a bad thing or planning for the future wrong. Rather, that fear should not be our master and that God's faithful provision should not only flow to us but through us to those in need.

Prior to writing this I held in my hand one of the few remaining jars still full of silver coins. Shut up for so many years, they seemed to want to speak, so I figured I would give them a chance. There, forged on both their sides was the simple message that has made this country so great: Liberty and In God We Trust. Perhaps it's time we tell the next generation about our secret and start tearing down some old walls.

*"And I will shake all nations, and the desire of all nations shall come: and I will fill this house with glory, saith the LORD of hosts. The silver is mine, and the gold is mine, saith the LORD of hosts. The glory of this latter house shall be greater than of the former, saith the LORD of hosts: and in this place will I give peace, saith the LORD of hosts." (Haggai 2:7-9)*

# Fire That Will Never Be Put Out

Billows of smoke rolled up the face of our white brick fireplace. With my face pressed close to the flames and cheeks full of all the air an eleven-year-old can muster, I blew at the burning paper I had so carefully stuffed under the logs. It didn't take long for the rolling smoke to fill the living room of our two-story Vermont home.

It was the first fire I had ever built on my own and I was determined it would be the best one mom had ever seen. Little did I know that before it was all over with, we would be filing an insurance claim.

Though the flue was open and paper and wood stacked properly, the cold bricks made it difficult for the smoke to find its way out the chimney. Cloud after cloud continued to fill the room as I did my best to save both house and reputation. By the time the smoke reached my mom, busy baking in the kitchen, all hope was gone of proving to her I was now a young man.

Like a well-trained professional, she raced to the cupboard and grabbed the fire extinguisher. With pin pulled and trigger squeezed, mom was forced to put out the very thing I was trying so hard to make work. The carefully stacked logs, representing in part my passage into adulthood, now lie cold and covered in white chemical powder.

Though handled very lovingly by mom, I had no idea how the incident would affect my adult life. From that day forward, every time God wanted to promote or bless me, I always drew back. It was years before I realized that a subconscious fear of failure was controlling my life.

It's amazing how each life experience has the potential to set the boundaries of our future. Waiting at the door of every success or failure are a myriad of voices telling us how we ought to view ourselves. Unfortunately, as children and sometimes even as adults, we lack the necessary skills to sort through all the thoughts that run through our minds.

It's for this very reason that God has given us the Bible. In Hebrews 4:12 we're told that the word of God is alive and powerful and sharper than any two-edged sword. It is able to sort through all our thoughts and help us discern what's from God and what is not. It's also a lamp to our feet and a light to our path, according to Psalm 119:105. Without it, we're just groping around in the dark.

Is it any wonder that the Bible still remains the most influential book in all of human history? Though Roman emperors have ordered its annihilation and millions upon millions of copies have been burned, it still remains the most widely read, widely published and influential book of all time. Not only was it the first thing to roll off the printing press, but no other writing has done more to shape law, science and culture in such a profound and lasting way.

As for me, its message of salvation and proper self-image have set me free from the snares of my past. I must admit it feels so good to be building fires again; especially the kind that never need putting out.

*"And they said one to another, Did not our heart burn within us, while he talked with us by the way, and while he opened to us the scriptures?" (Luke 24:32)*

# Learning To Live Wrinkle Free

My car door opened and in stepped a young man I had agreed to take to court that day. His slender build and traffic violation reminded me a little of myself at his age. "Morning," the young man said. "I sure appreciate you taking the time to go with me."

As He closed the door, I couldn't help but notice the dress shirt and tie he had on. Though he had followed my advice to wear them, he had not taken the time to iron the blue cotton shirt that was looking really rough. It was obvious he had borrowed it from someone and in his own mind was doing good just to have it on. Though glad to see him wearing it, I knew that its extremely wrinkled condition was not going to help him as he stood before the judge.

As we drove, I looked for a tactful way to address and fix the problem. Finally, I found it. In a sensitive yet straightforward manner, I let him know how good it was to see him wearing a shirt and tie. "The Judge is sure to take notice of it," I told him, "but it really is extremely wrinkled. How about I let you wear mine, seeing you're the one that's going to stand before the judge today?"

"Ok," he said. "Whatever you think is best."

Into a nearby McDonald's bathroom we went and made the exchange: his much-wrinkled shirt for my ironed one. I don't know what people thought as we walked in one way and came out another, but one thing was for sure: there had been a change. The young man looked great and was ready to face his problems head on.

As for me, well, let's just say there've been times I've looked better. Though I'm by no means a perfectionist when it comes to my clothing, I have to admit I was a little self-conscious about the condition of the shirt I was now wearing.

Sitting side by side in the front row of the courtroom, we patiently waited until they finally called his name. It was then that I heard Jesus calling mine. "That's what I did for you," He said. "I took your messed up, wrinkled life and in exchange gave you mine. I put on your shame and let you put on My righteousness so that you might be accepted in the eyes of the judge."

Somehow, in that moment, any discomfort I was feeling because of my outward appearance fled away. I could literally feel the love of God for all of us who one day must stand before Him in judgment. On one hand, He is a God of justice requiring that every wrong deed be made right. On the other hand, however, He's a God of great mercy and has provided a way for us to stand before Him in an acceptable manner.

This is the plain and simple Good News of Jesus Christ. He took on our sin and shame and we get to take on His righteousness. As for me, I'm so glad that over 30 years ago Jesus stopped by to pick me up and convinced me I needed to change my clothes.

*"I will greatly rejoice in the LORD, my soul shall be joyful in my God; for he hath clothed me with the garments of salvation, he hath covered me with the robe of righteousness, as a bridegroom decketh himself with ornaments, and as a bride adorneth herself with her jewels"* *(Isaiah 61:10)*

# The Power Of A Greater Attraction

With paws positioned like a set of human hands, the russet-colored Bulldog clung to its new found bone. His powerful jaws gnawed its end with a contentment that only a dog can fully appreciate. It seemed Butch the dog was always bringing something home from his daily wanderings and this time he had struck it rich. Perhaps from a neighbor's trash or nearby compost pile, the bone was a prize not often found in his neck of the woods.

The sound of teeth grinding bone and strange guttural noises was just enough to let the dog's owner know he was home. "What have you got now Butch?" the owner asked as he stepped out the side door and onto the wooden porch where Butch spent most of his time just being a dog. "Ok buddy, you better give that one to me," the owner said as he reached down to remove the jagged splintering bone from his mouth.

Though Butch had never bitten anyone, and was as loyal as a dog gets, the thought of someone taking his bone was more then he could bear. Somewhere from deep down inside came a threatening growl that surprised both owner and dog alike. "This one's mine," Butch seemed to be saying, "and though I respect you as my master, don't mess with my bone."

Shocked, yet still concerned, the owner drew back to rethink his approach at delivering his dog from the splintering bone. Then it hit him. Into the house he went, opened the refrigerator door and pulled out last night's leftovers. It wouldn't take much he thought, as he cut off a relatively small piece of steak and headed back to the contest waiting on the porch. With steak in hand and absolute confidence, the owner waved the piece of meat in front of Butch's nose.

Instantly the competition for the bone was over. With a gentle toss of the meat down the front stairs, the owner watched as Butch leaped into motion. Delivered from his need to cling to the bone, Butch had awakened to the power of a greater attraction.

We aren't much different than Butch when it comes to holding on to things that we think will bring us pleasure. As a matter of fact, we all have certain desires and cravings, and we spend our whole lives, like Butch, wandering around trying to fulfill them. Though not often talked about in many Christian circles, living a life filled with pleasure is not all bad. Truth is, we were created for pleasure. The problem, however, seems to be that we've settled for something less.

As I read the scriptures, I find two basic categories of pleasure. There is the pleasure of sin for a season (Heb.11:25) and then there is the pleasure of God's manifest presence (Psa.16:11). The latter far exceeds the former and has the power to deliver us from lesser things.

It's my firm conviction that one of the reasons we often struggle with letting go of certain sins is because we've not yet fully understood the joy and power of God's manifest presence. Yes, it's true, we all are called to resist and flee from sin; but I have found that without something better to turn to, we always seem to wander back. It's my prayer that the gospel we hear is more than just one that tells us to stop sinning. May we all awaken to the power and pleasure of knowing such an awesome and loving God!

*"Thou wilt shew me the path of life: in thy presence is fulness of joy; at thy right hand there are pleasures for evermore." (Psalm 16:11)*

# There's No Place Like Home

"I'm gonna run away!" my sister announced for all to hear.

"Ok," mom said. "Where do you think you'll go?"

"I don't know," Karen huffed, "but I don't want to stay here!"

"Well then, at least let me help you pack," said mom, as she opened up Karen's small Barbie suitcase and began to fill it with clothes.

Karen was about six or seven years old at the time and in case you're wondering, she has given me permission to tell the story. I don't remember exactly what brought on the decision to run away, but I'm sure it had something to do with not being able to have her way. With flannel nightgown still on and slippers on her feet, Karen did her best to not look back as she made her way down the stairs and out the front door.

"Take care," mom said, as Karen continued down the drive way, determined to get mom to beg her to stay. But she didn't.

My sister went to the end of our neighborhood street before finally deciding to sit down. How do I know? Because we were watching from afar. I can only imagine what was going through her little mind as she pondered the cost of her decision. Finally, after about half an hour, Karen decided that home was not that bad of a place after all. I don't know if it was the thought of what might happen at dark, or perhaps feelings of hunger, but somehow things began to come into focus. With suitcase in hand, and a somewhat slower and meandering pace, she made her way back home, this time with a little different attitude.

As one might imagine, mom did her best to appear surprised and was very ready to receive her back into the fold. As for Karen and the rest of the Goyette clan, no one had to explain the blessings and privileges of living in our home any further.

Though it may seem a little distant at first, the story of my sister Karen strikes a little closer to home than might be realized. From Adam and Eve to all who have followed after, the truth is that we all like to have things our own way.  God in His infinite wisdom is more than willing to accommodate us if the end result will bring us home with a different attitude. Like my sister Karen, we're all free to leave and experience life on our own. Each one of us has a free will and a choice to make.  If we think that living outside of God's principles and laws will make us happy, we're free to have at it. One thing is for sure, whether we agree with His rules for living or not, He loves us just the same.

I've discovered that God is a caring father, and though for many years I felt like I wanted to run away, I finally came full circle when I realized there's no better place to be than in His house. After my own season of sitting at the end of the street, a hunger for something more was enough to cause me to get up, swallow my pride, and return to the Lord. How wonderful it was to find Him ready to receive me! Whether we are near or far, or perhaps somewhere in between, may we be mindful that our Father in heaven is constantly watching and waiting for us all to come home.

*"And when he came to himself, he said, How many hired servants of my father's have bread enough and to spare, and I perish with hunger! I will arise and go to my father, and will say unto him, Father, I have sinned against heaven, and before thee, And he arose, and came to his father. But when he was yet a great way off, his father saw him, and had compassion, and ran, and fell on his neck, and kissed him." (Luke 15:17-20)*

# Finding The Meaning Of Christmas

"That's the one I want Dad," said the young boy pointing at the red mountain bike.

"That sure is nice," the father replied, "but at the moment it doesn't look like we'll be able to afford it." With no real argument, the disappointed boy shrugged his shoulders and gave into the reality of his family's situation. Though it was Christmas, the sting of mom and dad's divorce was still fresh upon them all.

Deep in the father's heart was a burning desire to buy the bike, but he wanted to be careful not to get his son's hopes up prematurely. Week after week he listened as all the children dropped hints about what they wanted for Christmas. Though the son still had his eyes set on the bike, he did his best not to put any added pressure on his dad.

With Christmas just a few days off, and all the children dreaming about opening presents, out of the young boy's mouth came the question he had been trying so hard not to ask. "Do you think we'll be able to afford it dad?" assuming dad knew what he meant.

"Afford what?" Dad asked.

"The red bike," the son said surprised that he'd forgotten.

"Well son, right now things don't look all that good, maybe next year."

"Ok," the son said as he slowly turned away and did his best to cover up his feelings. Little did he know that dad had found a way to buy the bike and was storing it in the neighbor's garage.

As Christmas day arrived and all the children flooded into the living room to open their gifts, the red bicycle was nowhere to be found. Gift by gift they opened their presents, each one receiving at least one special thing, except the son that is. As he opened his last gift, a small jewelry box, tucked in cotton was an old key on a key ring. Not quite sure what to make of it, the son looked at dad and did his best to give thanks.

"You're welcome," his dad said. "Aren't you interested to know what the key is for?"

To the boy's quizzical expression the dad said, "it looks like the key to the neighbor's garage door to me."

And then it hit him! With eyes wide open and key in hand, the young boy jumped to his feet and ran next door. As his father and siblings watched from their front yard, the boy managed to unlock the door and fling it open. There before his eyes, ready to ride, was the red mountain bike he had so desperately wanted. Abruptly, without even touching the bike, the son came bolting across the yard and threw himself around his dad's neck. Though thrilled about his new bicycle, the love of his father was of far more importance, especially in light of all they had been through.

This true story serves as a beautiful reminder of what Christmas is all about. God so loved us all that He gave the most extravagant gift that He could possibly give -- Jesus Christ. As we enjoy His blessings, may our hearts be stirred to put down all the temporal gifts and gadgets, and like the son in the story, run into the Father's loving arms and give Him thanks for all He's done.

*"And one of them, when he saw that he was healed, turned back, and with a loud voice glorified God, and fell down on his face at his feet, giving him thanks: and he was a Samaritan. And Jesus answering said, Were there not ten cleansed? but where are the nine? There are not found that returned to give glory to God, save this stranger. And he said unto him, Arise, go thy way: thy faith hath made thee whole."*
Luke 17:15-19

# For Those Who Wait For Him

As the living room filled with a few men and a group of older women, I began to ask myself what I was even doing at the meeting. Though invited by a close friend who wanted to introduce me to somebody, I was having second thoughts and wondering if I should have just stayed home. Although some of the best church meetings I've ever been in have happened in people's homes, my motive for being at this one was a little questionable.

Let me explain. I was single and waiting for God to bring me a good wife. Now I know that's not a great reason for going to a church meeting, but in part that's why I was there. Trust me, I did my best to put away all the words my friend had told me about the woman he wanted me to meet, but it wasn't easy. "She loves the Lord with all her heart," he had said, "and on top of that she is very beautiful." Well beautiful is good, I had thought, but what I really need is someone who loves God more than she would ever love me.

As the house continued to fill with people and the meeting was almost ready to begin, I decided to end the struggle that was going on in my mind. "Lord," I said under my breath, "if for some reason there's someone You want me to meet here tonight, I ask you to let her sit on that white chair across the room." Now please understand I'm not one for putting 'fleeces' before the Lord, but somehow I needed to put the issue to rest and so I did.

As the meeting began, every chair in the room was filled, except the one I had pointed out to the Lord. "Hmm," I remember thinking, "Looks like God wants me to stay single a little longer." And with that very thought, the singing and worship service began.

Then it happened. After about five minutes into the meeting, I opened my eyes to behold the woman my friend had told me about. There standing in front of the chosen white chair with eyes closed and worshiping God was the woman that I would one day marry. She had arrived late (something she still likes doing), but somehow, she was right on time. "That's your wife," the Lord spoke to my heart.

"Wow! Great choice!" I remember thinking as I noticed her good looks and obvious love for the Lord. It all seemed too good to be true. Had God finally remembered me or was I just delusional from waiting so long? Before the night was over with, I knew that I knew she was the one for me even though she didn't realize it yet.

While that was over 25 years ago, I still remember how hard it was waiting for the Lord to work out the important details of my life. However, I'm so glad that I did! Tucked away in the book of Lamentations 3:25-26 is a message of hope for all who find themselves having to wait. "The Lord is good unto them that wait for Him," it says, "to the soul that seeks Him. It is good that a man should both hope and quietly wait for the salvation of the Lord."

No matter what it is we might be waiting for, may we each find fresh encouragement not to settle for second best, but to hold out for the good things God has promised to those who wait for Him.

*"But as it is written, Eye hath not seen, nor ear heard, neither have entered into the heart of man, the things which God hath prepared for them that love him. But God hath revealed them unto us by his Spirit: for the Spirit searcheth all things, yea, the deep things of God." (1 Corinthians 2:9-10)*

# With Thanks For The Music

The lights dimmed and all over the building the sound of people talking ceased. This was the moment they had been waiting for. Years had passed since the famous performer had visited their area and people from near and far had come out just to hear him.

As the sound of a few remaining voices faded into silence, the announcer stepped onto the stage as one single spotlight guided him towards the center of the theater. His voice, clear, confident and full of honor, filled the hall with an introduction fit for a king. Then out onto the stage he came. Not a very handsome man but that didn't seem to matter.

As the crowd broke into a thunderous applause, he humbly bowed and took his seat at the lone concert piano on the middle of the stage. With only a few slight adjustments to his seating position, his eyes fell on the keys as one thought, and one thought only, seem to fill his mind: faithfully playing the beautiful yet difficult piece of music stored deep in his heart.

As his hands lifted from off his knees, absolute silence filled the concert hall. And then it began. Note after note it flowed like water rushing joyfully over carefully placed stones in a riverbed made by God Himself. As the entire audience rode the music down the joyful stream, both musician and listeners alike left behind a world full of problems.

Suddenly the tempo changed. What had begun as a melodious capriccio style of music had now turned to something very different. Each strike of the keys brought feelings of anger, aggression and even pain. Evil and good seemed engaged in mortal combat as beautiful notes struggled with harsh ones until finally evil seemed to win. As the musician pulled his hands from the keyboard, closed his eyes, and bowed his head, the audience dangled in the air. Was it over? Surely, he didn't intend to finish like that.

Then, as if awakening from a trance, his hands violently hit the keys and began cutting through the silence left behind by evil's victory. Each note seemed to cleanse the air from all that had gone before, until finally the music returned to the exact same joyful stream with which he had begun. As he gently let the audience down with the last few remaining notes, he smiled with great delight having successfully played his song once again. Rising from his seat and taking his bow, the crowd stood to their feet and cheered him on as he walked off stage and stood just behind the curtain, waiting to see if their applause would welcome him back for one final performance.

When Holy week and Resurrection Sunday is upon us, I can't help but think about all that the Lord has done. From faithfully coming to this earth and taking center stage, He has played the Song of Songs for all to hear. From His beautiful birth and life, to His sacrificial death and contest with evil, Jesus has successfully played every note necessary to set us all free.

Though history has well recorded mankind's response for all He has done, it's still unclear as to whether or not our gratitude has touched the heart of the One standing just behind the curtain, ever waiting to come back for one final performance. May we each play a part in welcoming Him back one more time.

*"For this we say unto you by the word of the Lord, that we which are alive and remain unto the coming of the Lord shall not prevent them which are asleep. For the Lord himself shall descend from heaven with a shout, with the voice of the archangel, and with the trump of God: and the dead in Christ shall rise first: Then we which are alive and remain shall be caught up together with them in the clouds, to meet the Lord in the air: and so shall we ever be with the Lord." (1 Thess. 4:15-17)*

# Pulling Down Old Curtains

"What's that?" my friend asked.

"What's what?" I replied, as I looked at him confused.

"That!" he said as he pointed to the dark fabric hanging over my bedroom window.

"Oh, that's my curtain," I said, realizing I had some explaining to do. The time was the early 1990's, and to be honest, I was just coming out of one of the toughest seasons of my life. I was divorced, and while in my wildest dreams never imagined such a thing could happen to me, it did. Even though I wasn't a pastor at the time, having the "Big D" word stamped on my forehead sure didn't feel good.

The curtain, nothing more than a dark green piece of fabric draped over a couple of hooks and covering my bedroom window, was in no way designed to make my room look good. Actually, it did just the opposite. During that season of my life, I was working shift work and did most of my sleeping during the day. The curtain, as ugly as it was, did a wonderful job of making my room pitch black so I could sleep. Though I had recently gotten a new job, and God had been doing some wonderful things in my life, for some reason I had never taken the old curtain down. As I explained about the curtain to my friend, somehow things just didn't seem to click.

"I understand why you put it there," he said. "What I don't understand is why you still have it there. You're not working shift work anymore."

His words, simple but true, exposed something in my life that I had no idea was there. I had grown so accustomed to living in my pain and finding ways to cope with the difficulties of life, that now, at a time when God was blessing and restoring me, I was still stuck in my past. My friend's words, though somewhat embarrassing, were like sunlight flooding into my soul and beckoning me to leave my hurts behind.

It's quite plain that God hates things like divorce, and trust me I know why; I lived through it. It's also quite plain that He loves people and if given a chance, He's able to pick up all our broken pieces and give us a fresh start. To me, that's what the Good News of Jesus Christ is all about. I'm not talking about minimizing the consequences of bad decisions, but rather about the mercies of God.

No matter where you've been or where you are, God loves you. If you're willing to turn your life over to Him, there's nothing He can't do. As for me, I've pulled down the old dark curtain and am enjoying the light of a brand-new day.

The Song of Solomon 2:10-13 gives a beautiful insight into the heart of God as He calls out to all those who've lost hope and feel crippled by their past:

*"My Beloved spoke, and said unto me, Rise up, my love, my fair one, and come away. For, lo, the winter is past, the rain is over and gone; the flowers appear on the earth; the time of the singing of birds is come, and the voice of the turtle dove is heard in our land; the fig tree putteth forth her green figs, and the vines with the tender grape give a good smell. Arise, my love, my fair one, and come away."*

*"Unto the upright there ariseth light in the darkness: he is gracious, and full of compassion, and righteous." (Psalm 112:4)*

# Falling And Getting Up Again

"Huh! Huh! Huh!" sounded the voices on the other side of the door. "Huh! Huh! Huh!" they came again, only this time they were much louder. As my dad and I opened the door and stepped into the open room, it was just as I had imagined. Spread out across the gym was a variety of young men wearing white judo outfits practicing maneuvers I had always dreamed of learning.

The instructor, a short man not much taller than the teenage boys he was teaching, approached my dad and me and stuck out his hand to greet us. "Welcome, Colonel," he said to my dad. "This must be your son."

"Yes, it is," said my dad. "This is Rob." And with that, I grabbed his extended hand and squeezed it real hard just like my dad had always taught me.

"Come on in and get suited up," he said. "Your class is just about to begin."

Don't ask me why, but as a kid, I was always fascinated with things like boxing, wrestling and martial arts. Though I never pursued any of them very far, at that time in my life the idea of receiving some formal training was pretty exciting. As I put on the oversized Judo Gi and tightened the white beginner's belt around my waist, I felt ready to take on a whole gang of bad guys, all at the same time. Suddenly the instructor's voice, a lot less sociable than when I had first met him, called the class to order and outlined what we would be doing. "Tonight, you're going to learn how to fall," he said.

"How to *fall?*" I remember thinking. "I didn't come here to learn how to fall. I came to learn how to do flips and trips and fancy moves that would help me defeat an enemy." But, as I quickly learned, he wasn't asking for my opinion. After some exercises and a few basic instructions on how to fall, that's what we did all night long. Fall after fall we learned to transfer the shock of impact by slapping our hand on the mat at the moment of contact. Amazingly enough, it really worked.

Though I left the lesson that night somewhat disappointed because I hadn't learned any fancy maneuvers, I've since come to understand the tremendous value of what I learned that night. You see, while engaged in the struggles of life, falling, like it or not, is something that we're all sure to do from time to time. While none of us set out to make mistakes, it just seems to come with the turf. Though there's a lot of good teaching out there on how to succeed, I've found that very little ever gets said about how to successfully recover from a fall.

Falling is one of those things common to man. Think about it: even Adam and Eve in their sinless condition fell. That said, it makes sense that we ought to know what to do when it happens. One thing I've learned is that falling, in and of itself, doesn't define who we are as a person. What really seems to count is what we do with our failures. Proverbs 24:16 mentions that a "just man falls seven times, and rises up again."

How wonderful it is to know that if we'll take responsibility for our sins, confess them and forsake them, we can transfer the shock of our fall onto Jesus and rise up again.

*"He that covereth his sins shall not prosper: but whoso confesseth and forsaketh them shall have mercy." (Proverbs 28:13)*

# Don't Let The Devil Steal Your Faith

"Honey, I'm home!" Irene called to her husband.

"I'm upstairs," Fernando replied, "and we've got company."

"I wonder who it could be?" she thought as she made her way to the bottom of the stairs, with no clue of what was about to happen. There, at the top of the stairway and wearing a hat from the company where Fernando worked, stood a man she had never seen before.

"Come on up," he said as he motioned with his hand, as if everything was ok.

Though it was not uncommon for courier boys from the company to visit the house, something about this one didn't seem quite right. As Irene climbed the stairs of their Brazilian retirement home, her heart braced itself for the unknown.

Then it happened. As she reached the top of the stairs, the man grabbed her and pushed her into the room where Fernando was. "Sit down!" the man said, as he shoved her toward the end of the bed. She sat next to Fernando who was tied up and unable to move. "Tie her up, too!" he said to his partner who had been busy digging through all their belongings.

"Where do you keep your money?" the first man demanded, checking to see if her answer would match her husband's.

"We don't keep money in our house," she replied truthfully. "What you see is what we have."

With that, the man huffed and joined his partner in digging through closets and drawers looking for whatever they could find.

"Come on honey, lets pray!" Irene said to Fernando, now in his early seventies. Beginning with the Lord's Prayer and then on to the 23$^{rd}$ Psalm, they prayed and quoted scripture like there was no tomorrow. Initially the two thieves didn't seem to mind much. As a matter of fact, one of them began quoting the scriptures with them as if to say, "Big deal! I can do that too!" As they continued on, however, he got very aggravated.

"Stop that!" he said, as he took out a long knife and held it to her throat.

"You can't hurt me," Irene replied. "The worst you can do is kill me and then I'll go to be with the Lord."

"Be quiet!" he snapped, this time a lot more frustrated. "Ok, let's get out of here," he told his partner. "And *you!* You're coming with us!" he demanded, pointing to Irene. "We're taking your car and we'll need you to get past the guard gate."

Into the Volkswagen Bug they climbed, with duffel bags full of all they could find, and drove on past the gate.

"I'm going to be praying for you," Irene said as they drove further and further away. "You really need to change your ways," she continued.

"We don't do this all the time," the partner replied. "We're just trying to help out some needy children."

Not willing to push her blessings any further, Irene simply nodded her head and continued staring out the window. Suddenly the car came to a stop in a place just outside of town. "This is it," the lead man said. "Time for you to get out."

"Aren't you going to at least give me bus fare to get home?" Irene asked them.

"Lady, I've never met anyone like you in my life!" the lead man said. With that, he got out of the car, kissed her hand, and gave her enough bus fare to get home.

Though not sure I would have my mother in-law's boldness, this true story is an awesome reminder of the power of prayer and faith that reaches beyond this temporal world and lays hold on eternal life.

*"And I say unto you my friends, Be not afraid of them that kill the body, and after that have no more that they can do. But I will forewarn you whom ye shall fear: Fear him, which after he hath killed hath power to cast into hell; yea, I say unto you, Fear him." (Luke 12:4-5)*

# Letting Go of Things Not Needed

With a great screech the door slid open to one more rail car. There, staring me in the face, was another load of old cardboard boxes ready to be recycled. From near and far they had come just waiting for us to convert them back into something useful. My job was to unload the large bales with a clamp truck and put them on a conveyor belt heading for the Hydra- pulper.

The Hyda-pulper is nothing more than a huge blender. Just add a few tons of used cardboard boxes and whatever other junk might be included in the bails, pump in a couple hundred gallons of water, and you're ready to go! As you might imagine, the 1500-horsepower motor that drives this blender is a little more exciting than the one you have at home. As boxes and other junk swirl, slosh and bob up and down, it's only a matter of time before everything in the tub looks pretty much the same.

Now while all that's going on, there underneath the spinning blade is an extraction plate full of little holes. Anything small enough to make it through is quickly promoted and pumped away to the next part of the process, the Vortex cleaner. Sound like your life yet? Well, give me few more minutes. The vortex cleaner is nothing more than a funnel-shaped cylinder, wide at the top and narrow at the bottom. Everything that enters spins so fast that it separates into its own category. Things that are heavier like glass and sand gravitate to the outside. Lighter things however, like plastics and foam, move toward the center and are washed away, making the mushy paper pulp just a little cleaner.

Next, it's on to the pressure screens. Like large pots with lids, the pressure screens do a really good job of removing any remaining junk. As the mushy pulp rushes in through the lid, it finds itself in the middle of a basket screen and under a lot of pressure. To make matters even more interesting, right in the middle of the screen is an agitator. That spins and causes the pulp to beat back and forth in an attempt to get it to let go of any of its remaining contaminants. If it does let go, it's allowed to move to the next screen and then on to the last one.

If, on the other hand, it's too attached to its contaminants, it's forced back to the previous stage and is given one more chance to decide what it's going to do. Eventually only the paper pulp that lets go of all its junk is allowed to move forward and be used for something meaningful.

In Luke 3:16-17, John the Baptist says Jesus, "shall baptize you in the Holy Spirit and in fire: whose fan is in His hand, thoroughly to cleanse His threshing-floor, and to gather the wheat into His garner; but the chaff He will burn up with unquenchable fire."

After wheat is crushed, it's thrown into the air over and over again, separated by fanning away the lighter outer shell that is not able to be used. That's what Jesus has promised to do. Perhaps you feel like your life is always up in the air or maybe spinning round and round and under a lot of pressure. Be encouraged: it might just be the hand of the Lord setting you free from things you really don't need!

*"It is good for me that I have been afflicted; that I might learn thy statutes." (Psalm 119:71)*

*"And not only so, but we glory in tribulations also: knowing that tribulation worketh patience; And patience, experience; and experience, hope" (Romans 5:3)*

# Haircut That's Never Out Of Style

Around my neck it went, and though I knew he would never fully choke me with it, at times it sure felt like it. One by one we would line up for the inevitable monthly treatment: Colonel Edward R. Goyette's custom haircuts.

That's right, my father was bi-vocational. Not only was he a highly trained and respected fighter pilot in the United States Air Force, but as a side venture he had his own barber shop. Sort of. The only money he ever made was that which he saved by not sending me and my two brothers to a real barber.

With towel tightly secured by a clothespin around my neck, and eyes beginning to tear a little for lack of any style selection, out onto the table it came. I can still see it till this day: dad's famous barber kit. I don't know just where he got it but he sure was proud of it. Complete with a variety of combs for cutting different lengths (though that didn't seem to matter much with us), dad's kit was state of the art for the 1970's.

The routine was pretty simple. Dad would extend his unusually large hand, grab our face just under the chin, and tell us to be still so that he could get things looking "just right." For me and my brothers, "just right" wasn't going to happen with a military buzz cut. Every time he would finish, my already bigger-than-life ears seemed to grow even more.

As an adult I've returned to a lot of the moral and foundational truths my parents instilled in my life. For some reason, though, I've never felt a leading to get another military haircut and don't think I ever will. I have, however, had the pleasure of giving a few of my own. I bet you can't guess to whom? That's right: Colonel Edward R. Goyette!

Though mentally and emotionally as sharp as ever, a severe stroke had left my dad without use of the left side of his body. While the logistics of life have changed dramatically, I can honestly say that these last few years have been some of the most meaningful years of my life, as I've had the opportunity to serve and give back to my parents. Though not expecting such hidden pleasures as giving my dad haircuts, the experience has been life changing for both him and me.

I'll never forget the day my mom first asked me to cut his hair. As you might imagine, a unique look came over both his and my face. I suppose my somewhat sinister laugh didn't ease his anxiety much, but with us wanting to save a few dollars, and mom having already made the investment in a state-of-the-art hair cutting kit, it was a no brainer: I was the man for the job.

With towel pulled just a tad tighter than it need be, I reached forth my large hand, which I no doubt got from him, and placed it under his now grinning face. "Don't move!" I told him in a military voice. "I want to get things 'just right.'" With that, we both chuckled and I began. I must admit that getting things just right had little to do with the length of his hair. Rather, it was about letting him know what an honor it was for me to serve him at this time in his life.

The Bible says in Exodus 20:12 and Ephesians 6:2 that honoring our father and mother is the first commandment that carries with it a special promise. Though I've only just begun to understand what that's all about, I'm forever grateful for the opportunity to experience it.

*"Children, obey your parents in the Lord: for this is right. Honour thy father and mother; (which is the first commandment with promise;) That it may be well with thee, and thou mayest live long on the earth. And, ye fathers, provoke not your children to wrath: but bring them up in the nurture and admonition of the Lord." (Ephesians 6:1-4)*

# Pictures and Unfinished Houses

"Come on in, Rob!" my friends said as they opened their front door and made room for me and all my tools.

"Thanks," I replied and stepped into what was presumably their foyer.

"We're going to be working upstairs," they said. "If you want, just set down your tools and I'll give you a quick tour."

"Sounds great," I replied, happy to take a break from carrying all my stuff. Room by room we explored what was for them a dream in the making. With only two bedrooms and one bath partially finished, the house was clearly a work in progress. As a matter of fact, in many cases you could see from one room right into the other because they hadn't been able to hang all the sheetrock due to financial limitations.

Though the occurrence took place many years ago and by no means would pass today's building codes, my friends had been living in the house for some time. As we made our way from one area to the next, I couldn't help but notice how creative they had been in turning their unfinished house into a home. From pictures hanging over see-through walls to curtains covering closet spaces, they had done a great job of adapting to their circumstances.

After helping out with a few projects upstairs and sitting down to a wonderful lunch, I found myself somewhat adjusted to their way of living. Even the pictures hanging on the bare-studded walls didn't seem so out of place any more. "I suppose I could live like this if I had to," I remember thinking. Little did I know that one day I would build my own house and end up stretching the project out over several years as well. Though we were blessed enough to hang all our sheetrock and paint the place, I remember quite clearly what it was like not having kitchen cabinet doors and a few other non-essentials, at least from my male perspective.

Though in no way being critical of my friends hanging pictures over bare-studded walls, the experience drives home an important point that I think is worth mentioning. It seems to me that inside the human heart there's a great ability to adapt to our circumstances. If life is tough and finances are low, somehow we make the best with what we have and find ways to cover up the things that really aren't that pretty. While in and of itself that's not a bad thing, there is a definite trap we should all be aware of.

If we spend too much time making our current circumstances comfortable and simply adapting to where we are, it's possible to lose sight of the end goal. We can settle into a way of life that God never intended us to have. Just because as children of God we've not yet been perfected, that doesn't mean that we should be overly comfortable with our current condition. Decorating our spiritual lives with outward trappings that hang over empty places somehow just doesn't seem right.

I believe that we're living in a time when God is getting ready to finish the work that He's begun. Though for the most part we've done the best with what we've had, it's clearly time for more change. That being said, let's not be afraid to take down all the outward trappings of our religion and expose the unfinished places of our lives to a God who loves us. He is standing ever ready to complete the good work He began.

*"Not as though I had already attained, either were already perfect: but I follow after, if that I may apprehend that for which also I am apprehended of Christ Jesus. Brethren, I count not myself to have apprehended: but this one thing I do, forgetting those things which are behind, and reaching forth unto those things which are before, I press toward the mark for the prize of the high calling of God in Christ Jesus." (Philippians 3:12-14)*

# Healing The Things That Hurt

Sharp bolts of pain shot through both my ankles. Everything in me wanted to get up and run, but as I tried, I fell to the ground. Something was definitely broken. By the time the ambulance got there, both my ankles had swollen beyond recognition. As a matter of fact, it was a couple of days before they could even get a decent x-ray.

I was about 13 years old and, like a lot of teenagers, lacked a little common sense. It was summertime in Vermont and I had jumped off a roof not realizing just how high it really was. Now I'll spare you all the details, but one thing I can assure you of is since that time I've developed a keen sense of distance and respect for gravity.

With both my parents (God bless them) standing at my bedside, the doctor broke the news. "I'm going to be as honest as I know how to be with you," he said. "You've shattered your right ankle and cracked your left one pretty bad. The best we can do is to operate and try to screw things back together, but there's no guarantee how things will turn out. Only time will tell." His words went deep into my heart and for the first time I realized how bad off I really was.

Though many years have come and gone, I've never forgotten the process I had to walk through. In my ignorance, I thought that after the surgery they would just put on a couple of casts and wait for things to heal. Nothing could have been further from the truth. Their plan was to give me two removable splints so each day I could have the joyful experience of trying to please a physical therapist. One that didn't seem to understand the phrase, "I can't move it any further!"

"Listen," they would tell me, "As far as you move these ankles today is as far as you'll be able to move them for the rest of your life." With that in mind, and a lot of extra pushing on their part, we would launch out into our daily routine of moving the very thing that hurt the most.

Here's the spiritual comparison. Once we've submitted our lives to God and allowed Him to put all the broken pieces back together, we still have to walk things out and sometimes it really hurts. Good things come to those who let God finish what He's begun. As in the case with my ankles, my future range of motion was directly related to how far I was willing to keep moving them in spite of all the pain.

It's my prayer that those who might be going through a tough spot would find fresh hope and comfort through the words found in Habakkuk 3:17-19:

*"Although the fig tree shall not blossom, neither shall fruit be in the vines; the labor of the olive shall fail, and the fields shall yield no meat; the flock shall be cut off from the fold, and there shall be no herd in the stalls: Yet I will rejoice in the LORD, I will joy in the God of my salvation. The LORD God is my strength, and he will make my feet like hinds' feet, and he will make me to walk upon my high places."*

# Freely Received Freely Give

"Once you're inside it's the second door to the left," the guard said as he handed back my I.D. When you get there just have a seat and we'll bring him out in a couple of minutes."

With that, the electric lock clicked and the steel door opened letting me into the cold, sterile hallway, which led to the visiting room. I'd been putting this off for months but at last I finally felt ready. As I stared through the Plexiglas window waiting for the inmate to arrive, my mind drifted back to all that had happened.

It was September 19, 2002 and I had just received the phone call that would forever change my life. Like someone dragged into a drama they wanted no part of, I was told that my 17-year-old daughter had been in a terrible car accident and had not survived. As you might imagine, I came unglued. A wave of shock and disbelief flooded my soul as the deepest pain I've ever known surrounded me and wouldn't let me go. God's incredible grace in the face of such terrible heartache has drawn my family and me closer to the Lord than ever before.

As I continued staring through the glass and waiting for the inmate to arrive, I must admit I became a little unsure about just how ready I really was to meet him. Though it had been a couple of months since he had asked, the thought of sitting face to face with the man who was drunk and killed my daughter was not an easy pill to swallow. If it hadn't been for the Lord prompting me and giving me the strength, I'm sure I wouldn't have been able to do it.

Then it happened – into the room he walked. At first, it was clear he had no idea who I was. As he sat down and looked back through the glass, I broke the silence by telling him my name. Completely caught off guard, he broke and began to cry in what were clearly heartfelt tears of repentance and sorrow for what he had done.

"I'm so sorry," he said as he hung his head in shame. It was then that words came out of my mouth, that if left to myself, I would have never been able to speak.

"I forgive you," I heard myself saying, yet somehow, I knew it wasn't me speaking but Jesus was speaking through me. Shocked by the words and unable to receive them, he continued through his tears to tell me how deeply sorry he really was. "I forgive you," the words came again. This time we both began crying together as the tangible presence and love of God filled the room.

That day the man who killed my daughter, though still very much in a physical jail, was set free. Right there in the midst of all his guilt and shame, Jesus reached down and saved him. The same love that had rescued me many years before had now rescued him. Though I had never been directly responsible for the death of another person, there sure were times I could have been but for the grace of God.

While it's true that I miss my daughter terribly and long for the day when I will see her again, and I *will* see her again, I find great comfort in knowing that death doesn't have the final say. And now one more soul has been added to the kingdom of God.

*"And when they were come to the place, which is called Calvary, there they crucified him, and the malefactors, one on the right hand, and the other on the left. Then said Jesus, Father, forgive them; for they know not what they do. And they parted his raiment, and cast lots." (Luke 23:33-34)*

# Cutting Things Down To Size

The bed of the delivery truck slowly tipped up as a fresh load of lumber slid half way off the back and leaned on the ground.

"Ok, you can pull forward now," my boss hollered to the driver who'd been staring back through his rearview mirror.

As the truck pulled away the stack of lumber crashed to the ground breaking the steal bands that had held it all together.

It was the mid-1980's and I was a carpenter; well kind of. The truth is I was just a helper in training. Little did I know that one day part of that training would prepare me for being a pastor.

With the sound of the delivery truck driving off in the background, my boss began assigning each crewmember their task. Mine was usually pretty simple. I was the guy who carried the lumber.

Load after load and stack after stack, often walking through sand and rough terrain, I was as physically fit as I've ever been. Though just thinking about it makes my body ache, now that I spend most of my day sitting in a chair, or standing talking to people, I sure could use some of that exercise.

Though I was young and in good shape, I definitely didn't want to spend my whole life just being a carpenter's helper. So, every chance I got, I asked questions and tried to learn something new. It was that very desire to learn something new that stopped me dead in my tracks that day.

"Cut a preacher board 22-1/2 inches long," shouted one of the workers.

"A *preacher* board?" I remember thinking, "what on earth is that?" After doing my best to figure it out on my own, I finally broke down and asked the question.

"It's a pattern board," I was told, "that once it's measured properly and cut to length, can be used to mark and cut several other boards the exact same size."

"Hmm," I replied, "but why do they call it a preacher board?"

"Because it never lies," answered the man cutting the lumber. Though I got a little chuckle out of the whole thing, I still didn't quite understand.

"If you need a bunch of boards the same size, why not just cut a board, use it to mark the next board, then give it to those who need it and just keep doing the same thing over and over again?" I questioned.

"The problem," I was told, "is that every time you mark a new board from the previous one, they keep getting longer and longer. That's why you need the pattern board," the saw man continued; one board that everything gets measured from.

Though I'm grateful for the men and women that God has placed in my life as examples to follow, the bottom line is, there's just no substitute for having a personal relationship with Jesus Christ Himself. He's the Pattern Son.

The book of Romans 8:29 uncovers this beautiful truth: "For whom he did foreknow, he also did predestinate to be conformed to the image of his Son, that he might be the firstborn among many brethren." It's wonderful to know that there is a pattern Son who's always true. May God help us all to keep our eyes on Him.

*"And be not conformed to this world: but be ye transformed by the renewing of your mind, that ye may prove what is that good, and acceptable, and perfect, will of God." (Romans 12:2)*

# When Things Are A Little Squirrelly

Up her arm it ran. In terror, my wife screamed a scream I'll never forget. With the power out and our windows open, I'm sure our neighbors heard it all. One thing was for sure, if there was ever a time for me to be the knight in shining armor, it was then.

The year was 2004 and we were in the middle of hurricane season. I'm not sure what storm it was (there were so many), but it was a bad one. Strangely, right in the middle of the storm things had let up. That allowed us to wander outside to assess the damage. That's when we found them: three baby squirrels whose house was in a lot worse shape than ours.

The violent weather had thrown their nest to the ground leaving them all alone. They were some of the most pitiful things you've ever seen. Soaking wet they huddled near each other totally exposed to what was sure to be a few more days of torrential rain and high winds. Our daughter was the one that found them and, as you might imagine, the one who insisted that we bring them into the house. We dried them off and fluffed their fur to make them look a little more like squirrels instead of rats.

My wife, mother, daughter and I all sat around the table discussing everything that had happened over the last few days. From the power being out, to a large tree crashing against our house the night before, we were definitely living outside of our comfort zone.

"God has not given us the spirit of fear," my wife had just finished announcing to my mother who was a little shaken by everything, "but of power, and of love, and of a sound mind," she quoted from 2 Tim 1:7. Though she was absolutely right with her theological position, what was about to happen would bring the truth a little closer to home.

The little squirrel she had been gently holding somehow had missed her message about fear and decided to look for a safe place to hide on the back of her neck. Up her arm it ran, sending her into a state of absolute terror. As I struggled to deliver her from her attacker, it was all I could do to fight back my laughter. Never before have I seen such good preaching joined to such a dramatic demonstration! I must admit my wife is a great sport in letting me tell the whole thing hoping something good might come out of it.

Fear is something we all experience at one time or another. Though this story is a bit comical, oftentimes things come our way that are not so funny: the death of a spouse, the loss of a job, sickness, disease, bankruptcy, etc. Thankfully, the Bible is not silent on such important issues. 1John.4:18 tells us "There is no fear in love; but perfect love casts out fear."

No matter what you might be facing or what has run up your arm and gotten on your back, I pray that God would remind you of His perfect love for you. Though you might be right in the middle of the hardest time of your life, you're not alone.

God has promised to never leave you or forsake you. May that knowledge bring to you a fresh embrace from the God who loves you so much, and as a result, drive out all of your fears.

*"Fear thou not; for I am with thee: be not dismayed; for I am thy God: I will strengthen thee; yea, I will help thee; yea, I will uphold thee with the right hand of my righteousness." (Isaiah 41:10)*

# God's Perfume Available On Earth

Into my car he stepped. "Hello!" I greeted him as he plopped himself down.

"Hi," he said in a friendly tone. "Sure do appreciate you given me a lift."

"No problem," I answered. "Where are you going?"

"Just down this road a way," he said, not sure how far I would be willing to take him.

"Ok," I replied, and with that began the drive that would change both my life and his.

It's been quite a few years ago since I had the experience, but every now and then the Lord reminds me about it just to encourage me along. As we began to drive toward Joe's house, it didn't take long for our conversation to turn toward the Lord. As I remember it, it was Joe who began to ask all the questions. Before long, we were in the middle of a deep and meaningful discussion about the faithfulness of God.

I learned all about Joe that day. He eagerly shared with me all his problems and, in turn, I was able to share with him about Jesus. As we made our way off the beaten trail and through a maze of dirt roads, we finally arrived at Joe's home. To be honest with you, when I had picked him up, I wasn't sure if he even had one. His outward appearance had all the markings of someone who was homeless. Worn clothes, walking with a bit of a limp, and well, let's just say it, he smelled really bad.

"Can you come in for a little bit?" he asked, wanting to continue our conversation some more.

"Well," I replied, beginning to feel a little pressed for time and wanting to get on with my own stuff. "Ok," I answered sensing the Lord's nudging. "Maybe for just a few minutes." And with that, we entered the little place that Joe called home. After showing me a Bible he had and praying together for some of the issues of his life, I made my way back to my car and waved goodbye.

It was as I began to drive away that it hit me. Joe's hard life and lack of personal hygiene had left a terrible smell in my car. I'm by no means a neat freak, I'm just telling you the truth. As I chalked it up to the cost of serving Christ and those He loves, the Lord spoke these precious words to me:

"He may have left his fragrance in your car," He said, "But you left My fragrance in his house." Suddenly I realized the great privilege and honor the Lord had given to me.

The Bible in several places tells us about spiritual odors and fragrances. When our lives are open and available for Christ to live in us and through us, somehow the fragrance of heaven is released here on earth. It's that very fragrance that pleases God and changes people.

Philippians 4:18 is just one example. Though I'm sure I probably spend the majority of my time emitting my own personal odor, more and more I find myself crying out for the fragrance of Jesus to rest upon my life.

I remain eternally grateful for the day the Lord came into my messed-up home and left His fragrance behind for me.

*"But I have all, and abound: I am full, having received of Epaphroditus the things which were sent from you, an odour of a sweet smell, a sacrifice acceptable, well pleasing to God." (Philippians 4:18)*

# The Fruit Of Real Worship

Onto the floor he went. "What are you doing?" I asked my son Joshua as he began reaching his hand under the display counter.

"There's money down here, dad!" he said trying to convince me to let him keep looking.

"You can't do that," I told him. "Now come on get up. The floors are dirty and I don't want you down there."

The truth is I was embarrassed. There was my son, about seven or eight years old at the time, lying on the floor in the checkout isle at Winn Dixie. With my cart full of groceries half-unloaded, and a line of people standing behind me, I did my best not to make a big scene. "Come on, get up," I said again as I continued to offload our groceries.

Suddenly up off the floor he came with eyes wide open waiving a quarter. "Look dad!" he said, "I told you there was money down there!" And he was right.

I've got to be honest and tell you that the kid inside of me wanted to get on the floor with him and see what else we could find, but you know that wasn't about to happen. "Ok," I told him. "That's enough now, come on and help me with these groceries."

"Can I go to the gum machine?" he asked as he pointed across the room.

"Alright," I said, glad to have him off the floor. "Just come right back when you're done."

"Ok dad, thanks," he replied as he ran off to spend his newfound quarter. As the cashier and I smiled gently at each other, I was glad to see that the other people in line weren't paying much attention.

Then it happened. While I was loading the last bit of groceries back into our cart, my son came running back anxious to show me what he had bought. There in his hand was a small gum machine ring he had gotten for his sister.

"I got it for Rebecca," he said. "Do you think she'll like it?"

"Yeah, I do," I told him, feeling bad that I was so embarrassed by his previous actions. "I think she's going to like it a lot," I said. "That's very thoughtful of you." And, with that, he smiled and we went on our way.

As the pastor of an interdenominational church, and as someone who loves to travel, I've had the privilege of visiting a lot of different congregations throughout the world. From very orthodox and liturgical formats to those that are more charismatic and freer flowing, I've found that every congregation seems to have its own unique style and way of expressing itself before the Lord.

I believe that God is more interested in the fruit of our worship than He is in the style. Like my son that day, prostrate on the floor, it was the fruit of his experience that really mattered. He came forth demonstrating the love of God.

While I'm not suggesting that we all lie on the floor as an expression of our worship, neither am I so quick to judge those who do. Like Mary pouring out her alabaster box at Jesus' feet, though terribly misunderstood by those who were watching her, may our faith and practice be judged primarily by the fruit that it bears.

*"But the fruit of the Spirit is love, joy, peace, longsuffering, gentleness, goodness, faith, Meekness, temperance: against such there is no law."*
*(Galatians 5:22-23)*

# Saving The Last Dance For God

Little girls' faces peered through the tent window. Dressed like princesses, they stood outside waiting for the doors to open. The occasion was Faith Christian Academy's eighth annual Father Daughter Ball held at the Ritz Carlton. It's one of the most precious events that I've ever had the privilege of being a part of. Watching dads and their daughters pull aside from the business of life just to spend time dancing and dining together is a sight to see.

When the doors finally opened and dads and daughters began walking in, I knew it was going to be another wonderful event. I mean, how could it not be? From little tiny girls dressed like angels, to teenage daughters in elegant evening gowns, not to mention full grown women whose dads were crowned with gray hair, there's just nothing quite like it.

As people eased into the ballroom and the band began to play, the atmosphere was almost heavenly. With candelabras at each table and beautiful decorations lining the walls, this year's theme was, "A night at Tiffany's."

While most of the people spent their first few moments looking for a table to sit at, I couldn't help but notice a little girl about three or four years old dragging her dad onto the empty dance floor. It didn't seem to matter to her one bit that there was no one else already dancing. Though I'm sure her dad would have felt a lot more comfortable with other people on the dance floor, for her it wasn't even an issue; this is why they had come.

Song after song the band played and as more people settled in, the dance floor began filling up. As I looked through the crowd, my eyes fell upon the make-believe clock that was a part of the Tiffany's Jewelry store backdrop that lined the back wall of the ballroom. The time on the clock said 7:20 and stayed that way the whole night. It really was as if time was standing still. God seemed to draw near and grant a special grace for fathers and daughters to share their love with one another.

Between having their pictures taken together, enjoying the buffet, and thumbing through the memory booklets where dads write little notes to their daughters, the night was a huge success. When it was finally time to shut it all down, the bandleader stepped up to the microphone and thanked everyone for allowing them to participate in such a special evening. "This will be our last song," he announced. "We hope you all have a wonderful night and a safe drive home."

Out onto the dance floor stepped a dad with his little girl fast asleep and resting on His shoulder. As the band played its final song, it was clear that it was the father who was enjoying the last dance while his sleeping daughter was totally unaware of what was going on.

I can't help but see the heart of God in this beautiful little story. In Deuteronomy 32:9 the Bible tells us that the Lord's portion is His people. Have you ever considered that we are not the only ones who are blessed by having a relationship with God? He actually gets pleasure from us! Like the little girl fast asleep in her dad's arms, it's not our activities that are the source of His pleasure, but simply who we are: His sons and daughters. I've found whether I'm awake or asleep there's no better place to be.

*"The LORD thy God in the midst of thee is mighty; he will save, he will rejoice over thee with joy; he will rest in his love, he will joy over thee with singing." (Zephaniah 3:17)*

# The Palm of God's Hand

"First room to the left," the guard told me. "Just have a seat and I'll send him out in a minute." For me the routine had become a familiar one. Wait for the electric lock to click, walk through the cold steel door, and take a seat on the hard round stool in front of the window.

As a pastor, visiting the county jail has always brought me mixed emotions. On the one hand, I hate to see anyone living without their freedoms. On the other hand, I've also seen where people who were headed for destruction have actually been saved from it by going *to* jail. As a matter of fact, many of them end up having a genuine encounter with God. Such was the case with the young man I was visiting.

As I shifted back and forth on the uncomfortable stool pondering what life in jail must really be like, he appeared. Dressed in bright orange coveralls and with a gentle smile on his face, I could tell he was glad to see me.

"How are you doing?" I asked as he sat down on his stool, which I'm sure was more uncomfortable than mine.

"I'm doing good," he said through the thick glass. "Thanks for coming to see me."

"It's my privilege," I told him, and with that, our visit began.

To my delight, the bulk of what he wanted to talk about was the Lord. From questions that he and other inmates had been debating, to personal struggles within his own life, he was like a sponge soaking up every available piece of truth he could find. It was then, while discussing the scriptures together, that he remembered a special request from some of the guys in his cell.

"If it's possible," he said, "There's a few of them that would like a Bible."

"I'm sure that won't be a problem," I told him. "How many do you think you need?"

"Well, at the moment about four," he said, "but I'll have to give you their names so you can tell the guard who to give them to."

"Ok," I replied. "Let me see if I've got something to write them on."

As I dug through my pockets looking for a piece of paper, it didn't take long to figure out I didn't have one. "Well, just give me their names and I will write them on my hand," I said. One by one, I wrote them down as carefully and legibly as I possibly could.

"Well, I've got to go now," I told him. "It's been great seeing you," and with that I lifted my hand to the glass and he did the same. "Bless you," I told him.

"You too," he said. "Thanks again for coming."

"I enjoyed it," I replied as I waved goodbye and motioned to the guard that I was ready to go.

As I opened my car door, sat down and began to transfer the names that were on my hand to a piece of paper, suddenly the Lord began speaking to me.

These are the wonderful words He brought to mind, found in Isaiah 49:15-16, "Can a woman forget her sucking child, that she should not have compassion on the son of her womb? Yes, they may forget, yet will I not forget you. Behold, I have engraved you on the palms of my hands."

Isn't it good to know that no matter where you may be, God loves you and is for you? May the power of the resurrection, which brings new life and hope, meet each one of us right where we are.

*"This is a faithful saying, and worthy of all acceptation, that Christ Jesus came into the world to save sinners; of whom I am chief. Howbeit for this cause I obtained mercy, that in me first Jesus Christ might shew forth all longsuffering, for a pattern to them which should hereafter believe on him to life everlasting." (1 Timothy 1:15-16)*

# It Doesn't Have to Take a Burning Bush

I had always heard that if you ever had the chance to go to the Holy Land, you sure better do it. Little did I know just how significant that first trip would be. It began as my wife and I were looking out over the Sea of Galilee from out hotel room in northern Israel.

As is usually the case, any time we've traveled overseas it takes a couple of days before our bodies agree with what time it is. We usually find ourselves waking up in the middle of night and unable to get back to sleep. Well, such was the case on that unforgettable night. As my wife and I sat up in bed having finally surrendered to the fact that we weren't going to be able to sleep, a strange sense of excitement and peace filled the room. For hours we talked and prayed as the windows of heaven seemed wide open over our lives.

That's when it happened. With tears gently running down our faces because of the presence of God and the sun just beginning to rise over the Sea of Galilee, a violent storm blew in out of nowhere. Thunder, lightning and strong winds turned the peaceful sea into absolute chaos.

Suddenly a bolt of lightning struck a palm tree right outside our window. Never in my life had I seen anything like it. The entire top half of the tree caught on fire. No, I'm not kidding! It wasn't long before the sounds of sirens began filling the air and fire trucks arrived to put it out. In the meantime, the same storm that had come so quickly had all but left leaving a beautiful rainbow in the sky.

Let me make sure you've got the picture. This was our first day in Israel together and right outside our window was a burning bush and a rainbow. As you might imagine, God had our attention. Though part of me wanted to go tell the firemen to leave the bush alone (maybe God was trying to speak to someone), deep in my heart I knew He already had. At least for my wife and me things seemed pretty clear. God was calling us to be a part of what He was doing in the land of Israel. Somehow, that day we both knew that we would be coming back many times before it was all over with.

Like the violent storm that came out of nowhere that day, Israel has had its share of troubles. The whole nation, though full of tourists, is in the process of preparing for the worst. With Iran vowing to totally destroy her and others just waiting to join in the fight, nowhere else in the whole world do you find such a contest over one little piece of real-estate the size of New Jersey.

As for us, we've decided to be a part of blessing her and praying for her peace, and would ask you to consider doing the same.

I leave you with the words of the Psalmist found in Psalm 122:6-8:

*"Pray for the peace of Jerusalem: they shall prosper that love you. Peace be withing your walls, and prosperity withing your palaces. For my brethren and companion's sakes, I will now say, Peace be within you."*

# Believing Is Seeing

The door opened and in I walked. I never thought things would come to this. There filling the seats of the classroom were several other students that were in the same shape I was; we were failing.

I must admit that joining the ranks of those who might not graduate was a tough pill to swallow. Though it was true I had missed most of my freshmen year of high school due to a bad injury, the bottom line was, my poor grades were my own fault. Looking back, it's easy to see that my priorities were in all the wrong places. I was more interested in being popular among my peers than I was in doing well in school, and boy it sure did cost me. Either way, here I was in Ms. Corley's infamous remedial English class. I'll never forget those first few days.

Ms. Corley, a modest woman who spent her life helping kids get out of ditches, had quite a reputation. If she couldn't get you through high school English, no one could. I was sure to test her abilities. Now please understand it wasn't that I was dumb or didn't want to graduate, but at that point in my high school career, I was just a bit discouraged. If it wasn't for my parents, and one visionary English teacher, Anne Corley, only God knows where I'd be today.

As I settled into one of the few remaining desks toward the back of the classroom, I had no idea how my life was getting ready to change. After taking attendance and giving the whole class some basic reading assignments, Ms. Corley made her way toward me.

"What kind of things do you like to do Rob?" she asked in a non-threatening tone.

"I like motorcycles," I remember telling her, thinking that would be an area she knew absolutely nothing about.

"Great," she said. "I've got a couple of good books you might want to look at for your book report that's due in a couple of weeks."

"In a couple of weeks?" I remember thinking, "this lady's got to be crazy." With all the other catch-up work piled up on my plate, it didn't seem like it could happen.

Little did I know that as I began reading about something I had an interest in, my whole attitude would change. While it was true that Ms. Corley had to prod me along from time to time, at the end of the day I made it and got my diploma.

On a recent visit to Vermont, I decided to look up Ms. Corley just to say thanks. Though I'm by no means some great writer, and marvel over the privilege I've had of writing a weekly column, I thought she would appreciate knowing that her labors were not in vain. I was right.

Somehow, she wasn't as surprised as I thought she would be when I told her I was pastoring and writing for the local paper. It was as if she had seen it in me all the time; and, not only in me, but in all the other young people that had passed through her door.

It's wonderful to know that though, at the moment you might feel like you're failing, God sees beyond all the mess and is well able, if you'll let Him, to get you where you need to be.

*"Why art thou cast down, O my soul? and why art thou disquieted in me? hope thou in God: for I shall yet praise him for the help of his countenance." (Psalm 42:5)*

# Bombs and Blessings

The earth shook as another round of explosions sought to hold them back. That, however, wasn't about to happen. They were Marines. Unfortunately, even if they had wanted to turn back, leaving was no longer an option. The naval ship that had dropped them off had pulled away due to a surprise attack from seven Japanese war ships. The result, the marines were stranded and without their supplies.

The year was 1942 and the place, Guadalcanal. My father-in-law, Fernando Floyd, was one of those brave soldiers that miraculously lived to tell the story. With four U.S. and allied ships already sunk and no immediate backups in sight, just surviving their landing seemed impossible.

"We were totally cut off," Fernando had told us. "Our food and ammunition were all but gone. Honestly, it seemed that we were going to die. And that's when it happened. I'll never forget it."

"While covered in the dark of night, we heard another set of Japanese war planes flying overhead. As we all dug in, preparing for the hellish explosions that always followed, for some reason, this time, nothing happened. All we heard was large thuds as big objects hit the ground all around us. It wasn't until the morning that we discovered what they were.

"There, lying among the thick vegetation, like manna from heaven, were packages of rice dropped by the Japanese. Somehow, they thought they were dropping supplies to their own troops but instead ended up feeding us. The miraculous provision lifted our spirits and carried us through until reinforcements could come. It was an answer to much prayer," Fernando told us.

Actually, the occurrence was not as unusual as one might think. All throughout our country's history there are signs of divine interventions that have not only established us, but also kept us from certain destruction. From the first pilgrims being helped by the Indians, to the fog that cloaked George Washington and his ragtag militia as they crossed the Delaware, it seems plain to me that we all have a lot to be thankful for.

It's easy to look around and see all the things that are wrong with our country, but let's admit it, we are really blessed. Whether you are reading this from a jail cell or a hospital bed, the bottom line is this: you have a lot to be thankful for too. I've been in both jail cells and in hospitals oversees, and I can assure you, that in most cases, seeing what they have would make you want to bow down and kiss the ground beneath your feet.

Suffice to say, as we all slow down to celebrate our thanksgiving seasons, let's not forget where we've come from, and Who it is that has brought us this far.

Like my father-in-law, Fernando Floyd, and all those Marines who ate the rice that fell from heaven that day, let's be sure that before we open our refrigerators and grab one more plate of leftovers, that we stop and give thanks to the God that has made it all possible.

*"Rejoice evermore. Pray without ceasing. In everything give thanks: for this is the will of God in Christ Jesus concerning you."*
*(1 Thessalonians 5:16-18)*

# The World Is Waiting To Hear You

The noise was an unfamiliar one. Well kind of. I knew it was my daughter practicing her instrument but something was terribly off. Now as a dad, I've learned the importance of being an encourager and not someone who is always pointing out what's wrong. Still, what I heard that day made absolutely no sense.

Finally, my daughter emerged from her room. "Hey Dad!" she said excited to see me. "Come look at the new instrument I got."

"New instrument?" I asked. "What happened to the old one?"

"I traded it in," she said. "Don't worry, mom knows all about it. Besides, the band really needed someone to play the oboe and I volunteered to do it."

"The oboe, is that what I was hearing?"

"Yep!" she answered with a bit of pride in her voice. "Come on up and I'll show you what I've learned."

"Ok," I said wondering just how long the learning curve was for an oboe.

As I made my way upstairs and into her bedroom, I could tell that she had been working really hard at playing an instrument that no one else wanted to mess with. "Just sit on the bed dad and give me a minute to get ready. I'm going to play *'O Come All Ye Faithful,'* she said as she flipped a few pages of music and straightened her back as if getting ready for a huge undertaking.

"I know that one," I thought to myself. "At least I'll be able to judge how well she's really doing."

And then she began. It was a concert that I'll never forget. Note after note, and pause after pause, she did her best to play the music that was in front of her. Yet, somehow, none of it sounded right to me. When she finally finished and looked up for my approval, she must have seen the confused smile on my face. "Your tone quality was excellent," I told her, not quite sure how to approach the fact that I couldn't make out what song she was playing. "It didn't quite sound like the '*O Come All Ye Faithful*' that I know, but I'm sure with a little more practice it's going to sound just great."

Then it dawned on her. I had no clue as to what it was that she was supposed to be playing. "It's not going to sound like what you're used to hearing dad, until all the band is together. I'm only playing certain parts at certain times." Finally, I got it. In my ignorance, I had totally misjudged how well my daughter was really playing.

I find the same thing is true with our lives. Just because certain things don't make sense to us, it doesn't mean that people are not doing what they are called to do. I appreciate those who are willing to be faithful to use their unique personal giftings to play the notes that God has put in front of them. What matters is this: God has assigned us all a special part to play in proclaiming the greatest message ever told: "A savior is born and His name is Jesus!"

Come all ye faithful! Play the part that God has asked you to play. Be assured, it's going to make a lot more sense to those who are still wondering what it's all about.

*"Now there are diversities of gifts, but the same Spirit." (1 Cor 12:4)*

*"But the manifestation of the Spirit is given to every man to profit withal. For to one is given by the Spirit the word of wisdom; to another the word of knowledge by the same Spirit; To another faith by the same Spirit; to another the gifts of healing by the same Spirit; To another the working of miracles; to another prophecy; to another discerning of spirits; to another divers kinds of tongues; to another the interpretation of tongues: But all these worketh that one and the selfsame Spirit, dividing to every man severally as he will." (1 Cor. 12:7-11)*

# Wrapped in Simplicity

"I'm not going to do it," I argued with God. "It's too risky." Somehow, my disagreement didn't seem to matter. The overwhelming feeling of what God wanted me to do wouldn't leave. As I stared at the object sitting on the small wooden table, the struggle only got worse.

The year was 1994 and I was in Sawgrass, a gated community in Ponte Vedra Beach, FL. The whole thing seems a bit funny now but back then it sure was a stretching time. I had met the woman that I would one day marry and, for those of you who know her, you know that I really married up. The truth is I was feeling a bit insecure. Not only was she a very beautiful woman living in a really nice neighborhood, but I was living with some friends and driving a little red Isuzu pickup truck. Every time I drove through the guard gate to see her, I got the feeling that they thought I was a part of the maintenance crew coming to fix someone's house.

Anyway, that particular night something very special was about to happen and I was totally unprepared. As I stood in the foyer of her home staring at the flimsy piece of metal that someone had placed on the small entry table, every bit of my pride was on the altar. "Not like this God," I wrestled, but somehow, I knew it was His will.

There, sitting all by itself and at this point almost glowing, was a child's bubble gum ring with two hearts on it. Yep, you got it. Unexpectedly to me, God wanted me to ask her to marry me that night with *that* ring. Just to set the record straight, God was in no way forcing me to do anything. Actually, I had fully intended to ask Christie to marry me and had been praying about how and when. To me, I had wanted to do it all up really big. You know, set the stage, get the fancy ring, find the right spot; do all the important stuff. But now this.

I have to tell you, the risk was huge and I wouldn't recommend it to anyone who's planning to propose to a future bride, but for me, it just happened to be the will of God. Now the outcome is pretty obvious. She said yes, a miracle in and of itself, but of equal interest is how the Lord has used the whole thing in our lives. That night we both realized that the foundation God wanted to build our marriage on had nothing to do with all the stuff that money could buy, but rather on love and on being in the will of God.

This story is a gentle reminder of what Christmas is about. Though God loves to bless us and to see us prosper, at the end of the day the outward stuff is never the thing that really satisfies. I often think about the little bubble gum ring when Christmas rolls around and I remember the babe wrapped in swaddling clothes, lying in a manger. How simple. How pure. How uncluttered. How accessible to everyone, rich and poor alike. For me that's the point - the love of a faithful God reaching down to save us all.

*"For unto you is born this day in the city of David a Savior, which is Christ the Lord. And this shall be a sign unto you; Ye shall find the babe wrapped in swaddling clothes, lying in a manger." (Luke 2:11-12)*

# Safely Equipped

Swish, ugh, swish, swish, ugh... "Wow!" I thought, "I'm really doing it! I'm skiing with the big guys now." As I slammed into moguls and plowed through fresh snow, my friends, all expert skiers, watched from the bottom.

Skiing on a slope rated for experts wasn't the smartest thing I'd ever done, but with friends like mine, always pushing me to new levels, I had to try. Actually, everything was going fine that day until the intensity of my skiing exceeded the quality of my equipment. Suddenly, my 1970's Besser safety bindings decided to snap free leaving me in the middle of a turn with no skis on. What followed wasn't pretty—at least from my point of view. I looked like a rag doll, dressed in coveralls, tumbling down the mountain.

As you might imagine, my friends got quite a laugh watching me go from skiing with the big guys, to suddenly having no skis at all. Part of me wonders if that's why they kept me around—you know—for entertainment. Either way, I'll never forget that day when I realized that my skill level had exceeded the quality of my equipment.

Here was the issue: the safety bindings on my skis were specially designed to release if the person skiing crashed. In my case, they released for a whole different reason: the difficulty of the slope I was on. Funny, isn't it, how something designed to protect us at one level can actually be the very thing that hurts us at another level.

Perhaps you're wondering what all that has to do with our relationship with God. I have found that every new level of Christian maturity requires a new level of equipping in our lives. Unfortunately, like me with my safety bindings, too often we launch out into new places, expecting great things, only to find out that we are trying to function in a place that we are not equipped for.

God longs for each one of us to become more and more like Him. He wants us to be able to ski down the same great slopes that He does and to do it without crashing. That being the case, we must allow Him to upgrade our spiritual equipment along the way.

It seems that living in this world is becoming more and more challenging. The bumps are getting bigger and the hills steeper. Thankfully, God has an answer.

Churches all over the world are becoming equipping centers. They are becoming places where people just like you and I can show up and receive all the practical tools and spiritual equipment we need to succeed. Not only to succeed, but actually enjoy the ride as well

Though I've not been snow skiing in a long time, the lesson I learned about being properly equipped to face life's new challenges has proven to be one of the greatest lessons I've ever learned.

*"Every scripture inspired of God is also profitable for teaching, for reproof, for correction, for instruction which is in righteousness: that the man of God may be complete, furnished completely unto every good work." (2 Timothy 3:16-17)*

# Pride And The Power Of Truth

"You're a liar!" the man said to me. His words were like a sword, thrust through my heart. What made matters worse was that we were in church and everyone was listening.

It all happened many years ago when I was a relatively new believer. A friend had invited me to attend a meeting where a well-known, traveling minister was going to be speaking. If I had known what I was about to get into I would have never opened my youthful mouth.

"Before we close the meeting tonight, are there any questions?" the minister had asked. Somehow, I had found the strength to lift my hand.

"I've been struggling with pride," I said. "I know that of myself, there's nothing I can do about it—God is going to have to change me. I was wondering though, if you might have some advice about overcoming pride?"

"Yes, I do," the elderly gentleman said as he looked at me with discerning eyes. "The word I have for you is not an easy one. Do you think you'll receive it?"

"Ah, yes, I think so," I said.

"It's a hard word but an effective one. Are you sure you want it?" he asked again.

"Yes," I said bracing for the unknown. And that's when the words, "You're a liar," slid out of his mouth like a dagger from a sheath. Thankfully, the minister didn't leave me there, standing in my pain for long.

"Brother," he said in his thick British accent. "I'm not here to embarrass you but to help you. The message you've just received is an important one for us all. You said that when it came to your pride, you knew that there was nothing you could do about it. Well, that's not what the Bible says at all." He then went on to explain that according to the Romans 3:4, that every man is a liar and only God is true.

His point was simple. Anytime our thoughts don't line up with God's, it's always we who are not telling the truth. That's why he was able to call me a liar. I must admit that it was comforting to find out that in the context I've just mentioned, every one of us is a liar. It wasn't just me.

On the issue of pride, I had said that there was nothing I could do about it. However, 1 Peter 5:6 says, "Humble yourselves therefore under the mighty hand of God, that he may exalt you in due time." You see, I had been believing a lie. God doesn't humble us—we must humble ourselves. Yes, God resists the proud, and, He may allow us to be abased, but walking in humility is *our* responsibility.

Just like our lungs were meant to breathe, so our hearts were meant to humble. By the way, humility is not some outward show, marked by a certain demeanor, but rather, it's the fruit of having a proper estimation of ourselves. Humility is little more than walking in the truth. So, if my heart puffs up, and believes that I'm something great apart from the grace of God, it's my job to pull those vain thoughts down, not God's.

As piercing as those words of truth were, they've done more to help me in my walk with Christ than hundreds of well-crafted sermons. Though I still struggle with pride at times, at least now I know what to do about it.

*"Then said Jesus to those Jews which believed on him, If you continue in my word, then are you my disciples indeed; And you shall know the truth, and the truth shall make you free." (John 8:31-32)*

# Running Home For A Blessing

Something was wrong. Though it wasn't clear what, the look on her face was unmistakable. "What's the matter?" her mother asked. "Did you forget your lunch?"

"No mommy," she said as she tried to catch her breath. "You forgot to bless me." And, sure enough, she had.

As the sound of the approaching school bus flooded the neighborhood streets, the mother reached down, laid her hand upon her head and, as her custom was, blessed her. "May the Lord bless you and keep you," she said. "May the Lord make His face shine upon you and be gracious unto you. May the Lord lift up His countenance upon you and give you His peace."

While the last words rolled off the mother's mouth, the girl's eyes popped open, a big smile filled her face, and she bolted back to the bus stop just in time to climb on board. With the sound of the bus trailing off in the distance, the mother found herself not wanting to move. She pondered the impact that her daily ritual of blessing her children was making in their lives.

That was over 25 years ago. It's hard to believe that my stepdaughter—the little girl that ran back for her blessing—is a grown woman now. Truly, the Lord has blessed Rebecca in so many ways.

What is it about the human heart that longs to be blessed? I see it everywhere that I go. From the slums of India, to rural farm lands in the Ukraine, to right here in our own town, people all over the world long to be blessed. I have personally stood for hours and prayed one by one for hungry souls to receive the assurance of God's love and grace. Somehow, the knowledge that God is with us gives us strength to face the day and that's the way it's supposed to be.

From the beginning, God never intended for us to do this thing on our own. That was our choice. You remember, don't you—way back there in the Garden—back when mankind chose to be his own god rather than have the one true God? Though the whole thing grieved God, He was not about to force us to do things His way. To have done so would have been to take back the most important gift He had given us—our freewill. Without freewill we are little more than robots with no capacity to experience love. Real love must be free to choose; anything else is not love at all.

I hear people all the time say, "If God is so good, then why are there innocent children dying of starvation?" This world's problems have nothing to do with a God who doesn't care, but rather are the result of our choosing to do things without Him. Though He provides opportunity after opportunity to bless us, at the end of the day, the choice is still ours. Like Adam and Eve, still greatly loved but no longer allowed to enjoy Eden's pleasures, if we think doing things our own way is where it's at, we are free to have at it. Just don't blame God for the outcome.

As for me, I'm grateful that the Creator of all things stands faithfully in His place waiting to see if we will come running back to receive His love and blessing.

*"The blessing of the LORD, it maketh rich, and he addeth no sorrow with it." (Proverbs 10:22)*

# What's That Smell?

My car came to an unexpected stop along the side of Highway A1A. The passenger door opened and a man got in that I had not intended to pick up that day. He was wet and dirty and to be honest smelled really bad.

In my rush to the office, I had driven right past him when the Lord nudged my heart to turn around and offer him a ride. His name was John and he was homeless. Just recently discharged from the hospital, he was still wearing his I.D. bracelet. Dirt and dried blood were on his forearms and face and for some unknown reason he still had an I.V. tap hanging out of his arm. As we rode together, I did my best to encourage him in God's love and grace and saw to it that his basic needs were met.

Later that same day I picked up my wife for lunch and she, like I, had noticed an unpleasant smell in my new car. I was quick to inform her of my encounter with the homeless man and that I would be sure to get some upholstery cleaner on the way home.

It was then, on the way home, that I discovered the real problem. There in the back of my SUV was the bag of trash that I had placed there that morning on my way to work. After a long day in the sun it smelled pretty ripe. I had thought the smell had belonged to John, but actually it was the bag of trash I was carrying.

God has always been faithful to speak to me through simple, and sometimes humorous, life circumstances. Such was the case with John and my bag of trash. God in His loving and yet direct way wanted to remind me of a few very important truths.

The first is that we are basically all the same. Though on the outside most of us appear reasonably successful at managing life and circumstance, on the inside we're all in desperate need of God. If He were to withdraw His grace and talent from our lives, every one of us would come unraveled.

I don't presume to know all the reasons why people end up destitute and homeless but I do know why I'm not. I can cite my hard work and the exercising of wisdom in life and management skills, but the bottom line is, like the apostle Paul, "I am what I am by the grace of God."

Secondly, John reminded me of the simple truth that when we judge others, we condemn ourselves. The Bible says, "Judge not that you be not judged. For with what judgment you judge, you shall be judged: and with what measure you mete, it shall be measured to you." Matt.7:1-2

I had not maliciously judged John that day. As a matter of fact, my motive as far as I know was to honor God by giving him a lift. Yet, somehow, even in our acts of kindness, if we are not careful, we end up offering a hand that people cannot relate to.

If our help is extended from some high place on the religious or social totem pole, we only rob people of their dignity. If, however, we come to them in humility, acknowledging the fact that we all share a common need, our help offers hope and grace for change. In essence we are saying, 'God has helped me, and if He can help me, I know He can help you.'

I'm so grateful that Jesus is still interested in picking people up, especially when they need a lift.

*"For, brethren, you have been called unto liberty; only use not liberty for an occasion to the flesh, but by love serve one another." (Galatians 5:13)*

# Science, Faith and God

Crunch! Crack! Creak! As we watched, it collapsed. The look on our teacher's face said it all. He knew it was going to happen. The classroom filled with wonder as the object in front of us continued to fold and crumble.

Of all the high school classes I took, science was my favorite. Though I was a bit distracted by social issues and as a result, not the greatest student, anytime we got to engage in a science project, I was all over it. From dissecting frogs to creating flammable gases, I found it all fascinating. Nothing, however, caught my attention quite like the day I watched the steel one-gallon can fold into a twisted mass right in front of my eyes. Nobody was even touching it.

Now please don't try this at home, but here's how it worked. Our teacher took an empty one-gallon metal can and washed it out thoroughly. With the lid off, he placed the can in a special holder and then put a small Bunsen burner under it and began heating it up. Once it was good and hot, he carefully screwed the lid back on and shut the burner off. The results were astounding. Abruptly, as we all stared at it, the hot can collapsed. It was as if some huge invisible creature had come into the room, grabbed the can in its hand, and began crushing it. I'm not talking about putting a few little dents in it. I'm talking about crushing it.

Our teacher, being the good teacher that he was, seized the moment. "Here's how it works," he said, enjoying our undivided attention. "By heating up the can, all the air on the inside rises out the lid. Once the lid is back on, and the heat turned off, no air can come back in. The result—the atmospheric pressure on the outside of the can is greater than what's on the inside and the can caves in.

Before that time, I never understood what atmospheric pressure was all about. Now I know. Not just through my science class but through life itself. Have you ever noticed how when life's circumstances heat up and all our inner strength seems to leave our bodies, how the pressures on the outside can literally begin to crush us? I have.

Thankfully, God has left us with a remedy. The Bible is very clear. If we acknowledge our need for a savior, and invite Jesus into our heart to be Lord of our lives, He has promised to take up His residence on the inside of us. The wonderful thing is that when life heats up, he doesn't leave. To me that's awesome.

Think about it. When all of life is crushing down around you, if you've invited Jesus into your heart, there's no reason to fear. The presence of God on the inside is greater than the pressures of life on the outside.

Sure, I know that even good church going people can crumble under the weight of difficult circumstances, but I guarantee you it's never because God has forsaken them. A more likely reason is because the place in their life that belonged to God was somehow filled up with other things. That, by the way, is not a word of correction to you who are reading this, but rather a public confession from my own life.

Either way, the message of having God, the creator of all things, dwelling on the inside of you by His Spirit, is both intimate and essential to having a life of peace and victory.

*"Know ye not that ye are the temple of God, and that the Spirit of God dwelleth in you?" (1 Corinthians 3:16)*

# A Musical Haircut

Scratch! Scrape! Buzz! None of us had ever heard anything like it. I was shocked as the entire school broke out into laughter, and to think, they were laughing at me.

In all my childhood I had never been so embarrassed. My face turned bright red as the man on stage continued to use me in order to cause waves of laughter to break out from students and faculty alike. It's a wonder I've ever been able to get up in front of people since. I suppose if it hadn't been for my military crew cut, (I forgive you dad) and being so close to the stage, I may have escaped the whole thing. Either way, none of that matters now. It happened.

I was about eight years old when the guest speaker spotted me sitting in the front row of the auditorium that day. "You," he said pointing right at me. "How about coming up here to help me out?" By the way he made it sound, I was going to be a celebrity. Little did I know that the reason he had chosen me was because of my buzz haircut.

By the time I got on the stage and walked over to where he and his newfangled electric keyboard were, I knew something was up. I don't suppose I'll ever forget those next few moments, though God knows, I've tried. As he placed his hand on my head and began rubbing it back and forth, his synthesizer made all kinds of funny noises. My bristly haircut served as a perfect prop for his demonstration. I'm not sure if it's related, but to this day, I blush quite easily in front of crowds when I say or do something dumb. Thankfully, I've learned to laugh along with everyone else.

Who would have thought, that as a kid, I would have been a part of introducing cutting-edge musical technology to the entire school? Who would have thought that the very thing in my life that I didn't like, (my buzz haircut) could serve as an educational tool to illustrate the power and wonder of something so new and fascinating? Who would have thought that one day all of the quirky things of my life could somehow point people to Jesus? I've got to tell you, strange as it is, I'm happy to have it so.

For the longest time I use to think that being a success was all about looking right, talking right and having everything outwardly in order. Now I see it differently. Success for me is simple. Let my life be a prop for others to see the power and wonder of God. That's it!

Like the synthesizer keyboard that day, people hadn't assembled to see me anyway. They had come to experience the amazing sounds of something new; something they had never heard before. If we can ever get over our insecurities, and our need to focus on ourselves, the possibilities for our lives are endless.

Consider the possibility that your weaknesses and failures may be the very thing God wants to use to point others to Himself. Though He never seeks to publicly embarrass us—He's too gracious for that—He does delight in taking the things we despise and turning them around to demonstrate His strength and power. As for me, I've learned to laugh with God and everyone else when it's appropriate. I never cease to be fascinated by what He can do through the frailty and simplicity of my life. (1 Corinthians 1:26-31)

*"For you see your calling, brethren, how that not many wise men after the flesh, not many mighty, not many noble, are called: But God hath chosen the foolish things of the world to confound the wise; and God hath chosen the weak things of the world to confound the things which are mighty; And base things of the world, and things which are despised, hath God chosen, yea, and things which are not, to bring to nought things that are: That no flesh should glory in his presence. But of him are you in Christ Jesus, who of God is made unto us wisdom, and righteousness, and sanctification, and redemption: That, according as it is written, He that glorieth, let him glory in the Lord." (1 Corinthians 1:26-31)*

# Staying Close to Heaven's Guide

Explosions, gunfire and mortars shook the ground. I couldn't believe what I was seeing. As foreign troops stormed the city walls one more time, our guide called to the rest of our group. "Hurry up!" he said. "We only have so much time." Having been there before, I knew the importance of sticking close to our leader. With every word he spoke the battle raged louder and louder. Suddenly, it all stopped.

As I heard their voices and looked over my shoulder, everything came back into focus. They were a welcomed sight. With cameras, backpacks and water bottles hanging from their bodies, they blended right in with the rest of the crowd. "What happened here?" they said, in awe of the bullet holes in the stone wall. And once again, our tour guide began repeating a small portion of what He had already said.

We were in the land of Israel and I had been daydreaming. Actually, it's not hard to do when you're following an Israeli tour guide. The sights, sounds and even smells of history come alive as they describe the events of one of the most fascinating places on the planet.

As I gently smiled at those in our group who had been lagging behind, I couldn't help but feel the hidden frustration of our guide. He had so many wonderful things to share if the group would just stay close enough to listen. It's a lesson that had taken me a few previous trips to learn.

I don't know for sure but that's probably how God feels a good bit of the time. I can't help but wonder how much I've missed out on over the years simply because I didn't stay close enough to heaven's guide—the Holy Spirit. I'm sure He's been faithful to fill me in on some of the details I missed while doing my own thing but, the depths and the riches of God are only understood when we stay close to Him.

Unlike my many visits to Israel, in this life, we only have one go-around. The things we learn and experience here are what we take home forever. We're all just pilgrims and, left to ourselves, we're as lost as the day is long. So, if you're like me, hungry to know more about God, and what He's up to in the earth today, it's time to cultivate a more intimate relationship with the Holy Spirit. He is comforter, guide, intercessor, helper, friend, advocate, the one who shows us where we're supposed to be and, most of all, He is God!

John 16:12-14 records these words of Jesus concerning the Holy Spirit and His ministry toward us:

*"I have yet many things to say unto you, but you cannot bear them now. Howbeit when He, the Spirit of truth, is come, He will guide you into all truth: for He shall not speak of Himself; but whatsoever He shall hear, that shall He speak: and He will show you things to come. He shall glorify me: for He shall receive of mine, and shall show it unto you."*

*"And, being assembled together with them, commanded them that they should not depart from Jerusalem, but wait for the promise of the Father, which, saith he, ye have heard of me. For John truly baptized with water; but ye shall be baptized with the Holy Ghost not many days hence." (Acts 1:4-5)*

# Knowing Who Is Watching

It's been several years ago, but I'll never forget it. There I stood on a Wednesday night preparing to minister. The truth is, I was a little discouraged. Though at the time I hadn't been pastoring long, God knows I was giving it my all. As I stood behind the pulpit to minister, I couldn't help but think of all the people who weren't there. I later learned that's a trap that many pastors fall into.

Thankfully, somehow, I was able to realize that those who had shown up deserved the very best I had to offer them. Besides, I had studied and prayed all day. To not share the precious truths God had shared with me, just because certain people had not shown up, would be a terrible disservice to those who had.

As I pushed through the atmosphere of empty seats and thoughts of discouragement, my role came back into focus. Whether there were many people or few, I was going to feed them the word of God. That's what He called me to do.

It wasn't until I finished teaching that night that the memorable event took place. An older gentleman who was present approached me and shared with me something he had seen. While I was ministering, he had had a vision. I know, for some that may seem a bit strange, but the Bible is full of such occurrences.

In the vision, he saw Jesus standing not far away from the pulpit where I was ministering. With one hand on His chin, and a large grin on His face, Jesus was leaning back against the altar and thoroughly enjoying the message. Basically, that was the extent of the vision. Little did the man know how significant it was to me. The idea of Jesus being present while I was teaching, and more importantly enjoying it, was a huge lift. And to think, I had been feeling discouraged by the lack of people in attendance

I've learned that above all else, no matter what you are doing, having Jesus present and enjoying what's going on is everything. As far as I'm concerned, it's the only real way to measure success or failure. Even the apostle Paul said that at a certain point in his ministry no man stood with him, but the Lord stood with him and strengthened him (2 Tim.4:16-17).

That vision has been forever burned into my heart. Whether I'm speaking to large crowds or small groups, for me, the important thing is that Jesus is present and Jesus is pleased. So, whether you're a pastor or a Sunday school teacher, doctor or librarian, housewife raising children or construction worker, it's all the same. If you are doing what you are doing as unto the Lord, He sees it and is cheering you on. In the end, that's all that really matters. Though at times human appreciation for what you are doing may be sparse, heaven is continually rejoicing over each act of service we perform in His name. So be encouraged, your labor in the Lord has not gone unnoticed.

*"And let us not be weary in well doing: for in due season we shall reap, if we faint not. As we have therefore opportunity, let us do good unto all men, especially unto them who are of the household of faith."*
*(Galatians. 6:9-10)*

# Snakes, Doors and Victorious Living

Her sudden scream pierced through the silent classroom. Fear, like a crashing wave of the sea, landed on them all. As the teacher burst through the louvered bathroom door, still fixing her clothes, terror filled her face. "A snake! A snake!" she screamed.

Over the years I've heard many stories, some true, some not. This true one has always made me think about certain spiritual principles. It all began during a typical day of school in a little one-room schoolhouse. The schoolhouse, dating back to the 1930's, was a warm and inviting building that had won the affection of both faculty and students alike. Though remodeled and brought up to current building codes, its charm and simplicity had been perfectly preserved. No one would have ever dreamed that just underneath all its outward beauty was a snake waiting to strike terror in those inside.

I can only imagine what it was like for the teacher that day. The idea of a long thin snake slithering through an unseen hole while you're visiting the restroom is sure to be a memorable experience. Though the snake turned out to be non-venomous, I'm sure none of that mattered when the teacher saw it gliding across the floor as she sat on the toilet. Thankfully, she was able to get her act together before exiting the so-called restroom; otherwise, the emotional trauma would have been doubly painful.

Have you ever stopped to consider how little unseen holes can create such big problems? I have. In my world of pastoring, we call those little holes "door points." Often undetected or considered of no real consequence, door points are openings that allow the devil access into our personal lives. In a spiritual sense, things like unresolved hurts, relationship issues, bitterness, unforgiveness, sexual perversion, occultism, unconfessed sins and the suchlike, all create holes that grant access to a dark kingdom whose primary purpose is to kill, steal and to destroy (John 10:10).

You show me someone tormented by evil and I'll show you someone who has been living with holes in their life. Thankfully, the good news is that Jesus Christ came to not only destroy the works of the devil, but to close up the holes that have granted evil access into our lives. As is the case with all the benefits that come from God, once we are aware of a problem, it's our responsibility to lay hold of God's provision. That provision, by the way, is not just about getting us to heaven, but about causing us to live a vibrant and victorious life here on earth. In the vernacular of this story, that means snake free living.

So, as a warm reminder, let's not forget all that He's done for us. Not only has He paid for our sins, but He's also provided a way to plug up the holes that allow evil to come into our lives at will.

As for me, though I've never had a physical snake slither across the floor of my house (thank God!), I have had a few spiritual ones try. I've learned that when it comes to having peace in my home, it's my job to keep the gaps and the holes closed.

*"Neither give place to the devil." Ephesians 4:27.*

*"Lest Satan should get an advantage of us: for we are not ignorant of his devices." (2 Corinthians 2:11)*

# Chum Bags and Stingers

"Ouch!" I said as I pulled my hand out of the bag. "Got stung again!" My uncle grinned slightly as he shook his head. He knew that eventually I would learn.

When I first moved to Florida, I was the first mate on my uncle's charter fishing boat. My job, among many other things, involved the wonderful task of cutting and throwing chum over the back of the boat. Around here, chum is all the stuff caught in the nets of our local shrimp boats other than the shrimp. To the shrimpers, it's mostly trash; to local sport fishermen, chum is a ticket to a day of exciting fishing. In my case, as first mate on my uncle's boat, Chum was a mixed bag of all kinds of stuff, some good and some bad.

I can't tell you how many times I got stung, poked, scraped, and cut by the diverse sea life that would show up in our chum bags. I also can't begin to tell you how many huge fish we caught as a result of the usable baitfish mingled in among all the other stuff. Without question, chumming, though messy business, is well worth the trouble.

When I think back on those early years of my life in Florida, the hot days, rolling waves, and bags of chum, Jesus' words concerning the kingdom of heaven come to mind: "Again, the kingdom of heaven is like unto a net that was cast into the sea, and gathered of every kind: which, when it was full, they drew to shore and sat down, and gathered the good into vessels, but cast the bad away." (Matthew 13:47-48)

I've found that life is just that way. Like it or not, there will always be some junk in the bag you have to deal with. For years I thought if I could just get the right people around me and manage my surroundings well, eventually life and ministry would become easy. Now, with a few gray hairs in my beard, I see things differently. Yes, without question there are huge dividends for having the right people around you and doing the right things, but don't be deceived—life is full of problems.

When I finally settled that issue, interestingly, overall, life got better. No longer was I living under some false expectation that at some point, in this life, problems would go away. Instead, I decided to roll up my sleeves, position myself to deal with things as they arise, do my best not to get stung, and get on with the important business of getting all that's good out of the bag.

While it's true that life has a lot to sort through, it's also true that it's well worth the effort. Shrimpers do it, sport fishermen do it, and most importantly, God Himself is committed to the same process. For me, knowing that keeps me encouraged along the way.

Though the context of Jesus' words in Matthew 13:47-48 is about the end of this present world and the separating of the wicked from the just, the principle is the same. According to the scripture, all who have placed their trust in Jesus, and not themselves, will be gathered unto God. It is then and only then, that they can expect to have all of life's problems to go away.

*"These things I have spoken unto you, that in me you might have peace. In the world you shall have tribulation: but be of good cheer; I have overcome the world." (John 16:33)*

# Crushed But Still Valuable

I'll never forget the time I found a $20 bill. I was just a kid, which made the discovery pretty glorious. It's true, finding $20 today would still be glorious, but you know what I mean. As a kid, it was like finding a treasure chest full of gold doubloons.

It all began while my family was riding on a ferryboat across Lake Champlain. For us, the trip was a practical one. My dad was in the military and across the lake was the Base Exchange. Anytime we had large purchases to make, whether it was food, furniture, or electronics, that's where we went. Ironically, the slow ferryboat was the quickest way there. Though I've always enjoyed being on the water, as a kid, the sluggish ride was a bit boring, until the day I found the money that is.

It's a wonder I even spotted it all, crumpled up and wedged into some kind of steel indentation on the bow of the boat. I've often wondered how it got there and why it is I even decided to investigate the strange piece of paper to begin with. It looked more like some kind of beat-up coupon than money. In either case, when I finally unfolded it and saw what it was, I couldn't believe my eyes. Though it was wrinkled and dirty, it was nonetheless real. I was in shock! Being able to keep it was even a bigger surprise.

When I think back on that amazing day, here's what I learned. Though the money was crumpled, dirty, and lost, its value remained the same. Interestingly, the same thing is true with us. I can't tell you how many times I've watched people get confused over this simple point. Just because someone's life is in a mess doesn't mean it has lost its value. Aren't you glad?

One of my favorite scriptures in the entire Bible is Romans 5:8: *"But God commendeth his love toward us, in that, while we were yet sinners, Christ died for us."*

I find that amazing. God didn't think any less of us because of our condition. Actually, He did just the opposite, and decided to show us just how much He thought about us by sending His Son to save us.

I've heard it said that if you want to know how much something is worth, just watch and see how much someone is willing to pay for it. That's a big deal when you consider what God was willing to pay for us. And to think; He did it while we were yet in our sins. The fact that God loves us the same, no matter what state we're in, is one of the most profound aspects of the Gospel message I know. If you don't understand that, chances are you will spend your life running from the very God that you ought to be running to.

I periodically bump into someone that feels a little guilty because they are not going to church somewhere. I've heard it said more than once, "As soon as I get my life together, I'm going to show up." I can't help but chuckle and grieve at the same time. God's not waiting for us to get our lives together before He loves us, and if you think you can get your life together without Him, you've missed the point all together. He loves each of us right where we are. For me, that's why I serve Him, not because someone is forcing me to, but because that kind of love deserves a response.

*"For I am persuaded, that neither death, nor life, nor angels, nor principalities, nor powers, nor things present, nor things to come, Nor height, nor depth, nor any other creature, shall be able to separate us from the love of God, which is in Christ Jesus our Lord."*
*(Romans 8:38-39)*

# Daily Tending The Fire Of Love

It's been over 25 years ago now, but the memory is crisp and well lit. As my fiancé entered the foyer and the pastor motioned for the congregation to rise, all I could see was her. Her dad, a quiet, stately man with tremendous integrity and highly esteemed by all who knew him, slowly began walking her down the aisle. It was clear that his daughter was one of the most precious possessions of his life and he was getting ready to hand her off to me. Every step they took together was slow and meaningful. On the left and on the right, for me, everything was a blur. All I could see was her.

Over the years as a pastor, I've married a bunch of people. One thing I've learned is that though all the outward trappings matter, at the end of the day, it's about the couple's ability to look each other square in the eye and, from their hearts, pledge their lives to each other in the sight of God.

On my wedding day, the beautiful woman walking down the aisle toward me and the vows I was about to speak were all I could think about; especially the part that said I would daily tend the fire of our love. I know, corny right? Well, not to her. Actually, she remembers those specific words above all the rest and every now and then reminds me of them (rarely, of course).

When I think about the wonderful relationship that I have with my wife, and the merciful God who brought us together, I can't help but remember why marriage, and romantic love, exist in the first place. From the Creator's perspective, it's a picture of a relationship He longs to have with each one of us. The apostle Paul in Ephesians 5 said that husbands are to love their wives in the same way that Jesus loved the church; so much so, that he was willing to die for her. Wives, in like fashion, are called on to submit themselves unto their husbands as unto the Lord.

If a man truly loves his wife in the same selfless manner that Christ loves His church, his wife's willingness to submit to that kind of love and protection is not an issue. Actually, in its rightful order; both parties come under heaven's blessing and pleasure.

Have you ever wondered why throughout history people have celebrated this very theme? From literature, to theater, to the big screen, the basic idea of a knight in shining armor, scooping up a fair maiden in distress, resonates deep down in the very fabric of our being. Though in Ephesians Chapter 5 Paul calls it a "mystery," at this point in human history, it really shouldn't be.

Jesus' sacrificial death on the cross, His triumph over death, hell and the grave, His victory over sin - and all of it for us - is by far the most extravagant demonstration of real love available to mankind. For those who've moved past religious duty and obligation, serving Him for love's sake is what it's all about.

*"I am my beloved's, and his desire is toward me."*
*(Song of Solomon 7:10)*

# Knowing Where You're At

Up the stairs and in she went. My wife has always loved exploring old homes. Usually, I'm good about opening doors for her, but this time she had beat me to it. Actually, by the time I got to the door, several other people had already gone in before me. It wasn't until later that we discovered our mistake. And to think, my wife was the one who had led the charge.

It was the 200th year celebration of Old Town Fernandina. Though Saturdays for me are typically prep days for Sunday church, my wife and I had decided to shuffle things around so that we could attend the event. Before I go much further, I should probably tell you that Christie is a history buff. That, coupled with her love for old houses, may have played a role in what happened, but honestly, the information we had received was a little confusing. Though our mistake was an innocent one, I do think there's something to learn from it.

The mishap took place right after leaving a wonderful presentation of the history of Old Town Fernandina. We rounded the corner and entered the house positioned right near where we had been standing. Everything seemed quite normal, except for the look of the house that is. With two cats lying around and a décor and design that did not appear very old, everyone who had entered the home with us seemed to be asking the same question: what was its historical significance? It wasn't until we left the house, and walked a little further down the sidewalk, that things became clear.

There, just around the corner, was a line of people entering a home that looked a little more appropriate for a historical tour. Though the revelation came a bit slow, when it hit, it hit in full force. The house we had just walked through was not on the tour at all. Yep, we had just walked through someone's private home uninvited. By the time the attendant, who was standing at the door of the real house that was open to the public had confirmed our mistake, we didn't know if we should laugh, cry, or find someone to apologize to.

Why God periodically lets things like this happen to me, I don't know. Maybe it's to keep me humble? In any case, my wife and I have decided not to take ourselves, or what happened, too seriously. Be assured, the thought of us going from room to room in someone's home uninvited, with a whole group of people following our lead, is something we won't forget or repeat anytime soon!

The spiritual applications are many. For instance, just because a door is open, that doesn't mean it's the right one to go through. Then again, we could consider the difference between sins we commit ignorantly verse the ones we commit knowingly. And of course, there's always the important lesson that says anytime a man follows a woman, like with Adam following Eve, you're sure to get in trouble. OK, now that's funny, but don't worry ladies, I'm just kidding!

In the end, I thank God that the door to His house is open to all, and to all who place their trust in Him they shall never be put to shame.

*"For a day in thy courts is better than a thousand. I had rather be a doorkeeper in the house of my God, than to dwell in the tents of wickedness." (Psalms 84:10)*

# His Life for Ours

The noise and sudden explosion were unmistakable. The F-89 Scorpion had lost one of its engines. My dad's Uncle Rob, the man my parents named me after, was in the pilot seat. His decision to not eject cost him his life, but saved many others.

As a kid, visiting my great uncle Rob's memorial was always a bit peculiar. The fact that it was located at the entrance of the Vermont Air National Guard, plus the fact that Robert Goyette was my name as well, always made me stop and ponder my own life as well as his. The details of his death have often inspired me and reminded me of God's sacrificial love for us all.

The year was 1965 and Uncle Rob was doing what he loved most -- serving his country and flying. Though the mission was a routine one, when one of the engines burst into flames, all that changed. In a split second, he faced the most difficult decision of his life. With only two options: eject, or attempt to fly the struggling aircraft away from the residential area, he chose to save others rather than himself.

By the time his interceptor aircraft touched the ground, it was too late. There, while rolling across the rugged field, he ran straight into a drainage ditch. Instantly, his plane nosed down, flipped up, and burst into flames. Though I was only a year old when it happened, the echo of the tragedy rang for years to come. By the time I was old enough to understand things, the message of my great uncle's death could still be heard.

I can't help but think about the love of God and the sacrifice of Jesus Christ. At a time when He could have easily bailed out from His mission and saved His own life, He thought about us. The fact of the matter is, in His case, dying *was* His mission.

Every year around Resurrection Day, I like to slow things down in order to remember. Like the echo of my great uncle Rob's death, though now a bit faint, the sound of Jesus' death, burial, and resurrection continues to shake the entire earth. Never before and never again will there be such a pure and powerful sacrifice. By it, not only is there forgiveness of sins, but in His resurrection, eternal life for all who believe.

If perhaps you're reading this and in your heart you're just not sure what you believe, let me encourage you. Though the idea of a resurrection may seem farfetched, when you put it in the list of things a loving and powerful God might do, it makes perfect sense. If Death is our greatest enemy, and God our greatest friend, is it any wonder that dealing with our sin and conquering death would be His top priority?

Though I realize there are many different ways to celebrate Jesus' death and resurrection, at the end of it all, there's only one message that really counts. I pray God will give us all ears to hear it afresh.

*"For God so loved the world, that He gave His only begotten Son, that whosoever believeth in Him should not perish, but have everlasting life." (John 3:16)*

*"What shall we then say to these things? If God be for us, who can be against us? He that spared not his own Son, but delivered him up for us all, how shall he not with him also freely give us all things?" (Romans 8:31-32)*

# Talking To Strangers

"Who were you just talking to?" His sharp voice startled me. In my gut, I knew I should keep walking. Ignoring him wasn't easy. "Hey!" he demanded again. "I'm talking to you!" Still, something didn't seem right. If it hadn't been for the badge he was waiving, I wouldn't have thought twice about stopping.

At that time, Nairobi, Kenya was one of the most dangerous cities in the world. Its nickname, "Nairobbery," was well earned. I was alone, and well, a little ignorant. With thousands of people clogging its streets, one obnoxious man didn't seem that big a threat. On the other hand, one obnoxious man waiving a badge did have me wondering.

"Who was that you were talking to?" he demanded.

Finally, I replied. "Someone I bought a sandwich for." My short, crisp, answer surprised him.

Quickly he recovered and pressed for more information. "How do you know him? Come over here so I can talk to you!" he persisted.

For a moment, I almost caved in. If it hadn't been for the little guy in my gut jumping up and down and saying "Get out of here!" there's no telling how things would have turned. With my hotel now within sight, I decided to keep walking. The armed security guard at the hotel's door somehow seemed the answer to all my problems. As the stranger persisted, waiving his badge in my face, I too persisted toward what I knew to be legitimate and trustworthy authority.

Ultimately, my persistence paid off. The closer I got to the hotel and the security officer standing at its door, the less confident the man following me became. In time, his so-called authority collapsed. His charade was over. For me, watching him turn back into the swarm of people was a huge relief. The little guy leaping in my gut thought so too.

I later learned the technique was a common one. A counterfeit badge, a bold approach, and an attempt to get you to pull aside for questioning; all of it a plot to rip you off. It reminds me of how the devil seeks to steal from us.

Masquerading as a real authority, his questionings always have an agenda attached. Anytime we follow his demands, the trap is set. Pull aside, and he has you. The remedy: just like what I did that day, put your eye on what you know to be true and keep walking. If the voices that are talking to you are legitimate, they'll have no problem following you toward other legitimate authority. If they're not, eventually, they'll flee.

Scripturally speaking it goes like this: "Submit yourselves therefore to God. Resist the devil, and he will flee from you." (James 4:7) I find a direct connection between these two ideas. Like my focusing on the hotel's armed security guard that day, focusing on God is always the right thing to do. The closer we get to Him, the clearer the wiles of the devil become. Actually, submitting to God is what empowers us to resist the devil and all his evil deeds.

Though it's been some time since I've been back to Nairobi, being accosted by lying voices continues. Thankfully, that day I learned what to do, instead of a valuable lesson. Submit to what you know to be true and keep walking toward it. In time, what is true will remain. What is not will flee.

*"Beloved, believe not every spirit, but try the spirits whether they are of God: because many false prophets are gone out into the world."*
*(1 John 4:1)*

# Italy, Art, And On To Perfection

A trip to Italy! Wow! For years my wife had dreamed of seeing the places she studied about in college. Watching her drink deep from the rich history and beautiful art was a pleasure all its own. Though I'm not much of a photographer, I took over 1,600 pictures. I just couldn't help it. Around every corner, there was something amazing to see .

From buildings, to statues, to fountains, to mosaics, I must admit that by the end of the trip, I was on overload. Now that I'm home, and surrounded by America's meager 275 years of history, I find myself reminiscing and appreciating all that we saw. It really was incredible.

Along with all the stunning architecture, I found the works of Michelangelo the most captivating. I especially enjoyed learning a few things about him. In particular, his philosophy for creating sculptures. The way he saw it, inside every block of marble was a prisoner waiting to be released. As a sculptor, his job was to set that person free.

More than once, we saw sculptures not completed due to funding that had been cut off before the projects were done. To see blocks of stone with the shapes of men beginning to emerge, but so much of them still hidden by areas not yet chiseled, really illustrated the 'prisoner in the stone' concept clearly. While looking at them, and listening to our guide explain the laborious process, the Lord began speaking to me.

"That's what I'm doing with you," He said to my heart. "With every blow of my hammer and chisel, I'm releasing you from the captivity of all the unnecessary stuff in your life. Though it's slow work, and sometimes painful, you can be sure I've paid in full to guarantee the project gets finished." I knew He was speaking of the price paid by the death of His Son on the cross. Those words flooded my soul with peace and joy.

To see the finished works of Michelangelo, his statue of David and the Pieta, and to marvel at his incredible talent, then to consider how even more skilled God Himself is, made me excited about the work He was doing in my life. Though I don't consider myself completely free from the stone yet, I'm a lot further along today than when He first began.

At one point, while gazing at an intricate detail of one of the statues, I found myself considering how long it must have taken to finish that particular feature. When I translated the idea over to my own life, and considered certain areas that God seems to work on longer than others, it all made sense.

He's committed to our perfection. Though He may have worked on something years ago with a big chisel, it should not be strange that now He's using a more precise instrument to get the same area smooth. For me, this is really encouraging. All the chiseling, scraping, and rubbing of grit over our lives is not in vain. Knowing that makes surrendering to Him, and the process of our perfection, really exciting.

*"Therefore leaving the principles of the doctrine of Christ, let us go on to perfection...." (Hebrews 6:1)*

# Tuscany Vineyards

Tuscany. Little did I know how God would use such a beautiful place. I'm sure the man sitting across the table from me would say the same thing. When I think about all that God had to do to set the moment up, I'm still amazed.

Nestled among its rolling hills, olive trees, and vineyards, the family farm was a welcomed sight for us all. It had been a long day. The wine cellar, now converted into a dining spot, with its aged bricks and warm wooden beams, made the perfect place for hearts to open and God to speak. Like putting on a pair of well-worn jeans, our tour group eased into the room, slid out chairs, and made ourselves at home.

Now only God knows why my mind works the way it does, but when the host began explaining how they produced such quality wines and olive oils, instantly my ears perked up. "In the long dry summers, when the vines appear to be dying of thirst, we intentionally don't give them any water. We make them suffer," the host said jokingly yet he was serious. "The result is a much sweeter wine. Because the vine reaches deeper to get what it needs, the quality of the grape increases."

Immediately those words translated into a truth I've observed for many years. Difficult places and times of suffering, in the end, often produce the sweetest things in life. Because such times force us to dig deeper, if we look to God, He uses the pain to create a new depth in us.

Little did I know just how that truth was playing out in the life of the man sitting across the table from me. He, being one of Australia's leading radio voices, had recently lost a son in a car accident. Actually, not only had he, but the couple beside him had as well. I shared my story of the loss of my daughter and how God had met me in all of my pain. Like thirsty vines, I could tangibly feel the roots of their souls reaching for the same source of water that had sustained me. That source is Christ.

Though I'm convinced that God is not the author of such suffering, at times He will allow what He can prevent if the end product is something eternal and meaningful. I realize it's a tough subject, and that some may not agree, but I've lived it and found it to be true. God can take the driest and most heart wrenching seasons of life and turn them for our good, if only we will search for Him with all our hearts.

*"Weeping may endure for a night, but joy comes in the morning."* *(Psalms 30:5b)*

*"To appoint unto them that mourn in Zion, to give unto them beauty for ashes, the oil of joy for mourning, the garment of praise for the spirit of heaviness; that they might be called trees of righteousness, the planting of the Lord, that He might be glorified." (Isaiah 61:3)*

# Stuck and Reaching for More

Panic struck as she tried the knob again. Nothing. Something was wrong. This couldn't be happening, she told herself. The woman hated cramped spaces. The idea of being stuck in one was terrifying. The more she struggled, the worse things got. Fear filled the entire stall until finally she exploded. Everyone heard her cry. To her relief, though still trapped, at least now she knew her tour group would not be leaving without her.

On the few occasions when I've taken tours, I've always wondered what being a tour guide must be like. On my recent trip, I think I figured it out. It's a lot like pastoring. As I watched our guide do his best to accommodate all the needs of our group, while repeatedly focusing us on where we were, and why it mattered, I thanked God that our guide was in charge and not me.

When I happened to hear his story of the woman that got stuck in the bathroom, I had to chuckle. No doubt, through the incident, he learned a few lessons. If I had to guess what those lessons might be, I'd say this. Loving people wherever you find them, and choosing to laugh instead of complain, makes the tour better for everyone involved. Somehow, that seems like good advice for us all.

If our guide hadn't got on the floor, squeezed under the door, and unlocked it for her, there's no telling what the poor woman might have done. When he learned that she belonged to another tour group, his momentary frustration level rose to an entirely new level. No doubt, his willingness to slide his fancy Italian clothes across a bathroom floor was because he thought she was one of his.

When he found out she wasn't, it really didn't matter. They both were in the same place wanting the same thing—to get out and get on with life. The message I got from the whole thing was pretty clear.

When it comes to helping people, our lens needs to be a lot wider than only our particular group. Whether were talking about our church affiliation, social economic status, political party, ethnic group or nationality, the bottom line is this: God loves people, no matter where they are and no matter what group they belong to. His heart is especially toward those who are stuck.

I know that as individuals it's impossible for us to help everyone on our own, but each of us does have a certain reach. The question is, are we willing to stoop for others, risk getting dirty, and meet them where they are? Without question, that's what Jesus did for us all.

With the elections just behind us, and a tendency for various groups to be more polarized than ever, I've decided to put my eyes on a kingdom that operates on a higher set of laws. Laws that were here before any of us and that will continue for all eternity. By them, all things were created and by them, we all can be free.

*"In the beginning was the Word, and the Word was with God, and the Word was God. The same was in the beginning with God. All things were made by Him; and without Him was not anything made that was made. In Him was life, and the life was the light of men." (John 1:1-4)*

# Tipping the Tower of Pisa

Of all the sights we saw in Italy, the Leaning Tower of Pisa was one of the most amazing. I never realized just how big it was. When we first saw it, my wife thought it looked like a huge elegant wedding cake. For me, I pondered just how long it would take before it crashed.

When our guide explained how the tower got that way, and what they did to stop it from leaning anymore, his words pulled my eyes off the tower and on to him. Having once been a builder by trade, understanding why the tower was leaning was easy. The ground was soft, and it didn't have a proper foundation.

When it came to how they had stopped it from falling, that I found interesting. After intensive calculations, the strategic removal of some earth, and by adding 800 tons of lead counter weights, the tower was stopped from its slow but steady fall. In addition, the engineers recommended straightening the tower to relieve some of the intense pressure it was under.

Though the people of Pisa agreed to it, they didn't want to straighten it completely. The reason was obvious. Tourism. If they totally fixed it, Pisa's popularity would quickly fade. It reminds me of what happens with some people. There's no doubt they are crashing, and need help, but ultimately, they don't want to be fixed; just preserved.

Often the reason is that they've learned how to get attention through the very things that are destroying them. To fix those areas would mean letting go of something that appears to be helping them. When we allow our current failures to define who we really are, we error. In essence, what we are saying is, 'God meant me to be this way and I should learn to celebrate it.' Sadly, nothing could be further from the truth. Though letting go of a false self-image and certain false securities can be scary, it's nowhere near as bad as living a life of constant strain and stress as a result of being so far out of balance.

When I think about giving up false securities in order to receive God's help, I go right to the story of blind Bartimaeus in the Bible. Clinging to his beggar's cloak, a sort of status symbol used to solicit money from the people, the day Jesus called to him, Bartimaeus threw off his cloak and reached for something more—God Himself. When Jesus saw that he was not just asking for temporary relief through a monetary gift, but rather wanted healing, Bartimaeus' life was forever changed. God opened his blind eyes and let him see himself the way God intended him to be!

That, by the way, is basically the same thing that happened to me. Bound up in a false self-image, I was trying to get attention through all the wrong stuff. Like the Tower of Pisa crashing, only at a much faster rate, I was a mess the day I heard Jesus calling. On that day, tired of all the dysfunction and pain, I threw off the old tattered cloak I was clinging to and laid hold of God. Without question, following Him has been the best decision I've ever made.

*"And Jesus stood still, and commanded him to be called. And they call the blind man, saying unto him, Be of good comfort, rise; He calls you. And he, casting away his garment, rose, and came to Jesus."*
*(Mark 10:49-50)*

# Waiting For Things You Love

On one particular day, I spent 12 hours with my son-in-law chasing fish. As if that wasn't enough, the next day we did it again, only not quite as long because of a family gathering that night. It was then, on that second day of fishing, that some unsuspecting words fell from my mouth. Initially, the words were no big deal, but once God got a hold of them, all that changed.

"You've really got to love fishing to spend so much time waiting for a fish to bite," I had said, breaking a season of silence. No sooner had those words come out of my mouth than I heard the Lord speak to my heart. "Amen—you'll wait for the things you love, won't you?" Though His tone was not condemning, I couldn't help but feel convicted.

There I was, gladly spending hour upon hour waiting for a silly fish to bite, but when it came to patiently sitting in prayer, waiting for God to talk to me, my patience level was nowhere near as long. Again, God was not condemning me, just agreeing with my simple words about waiting for the things we love. Since that time, that truth has changed my life.

As a pastor, a subtle trap is that prayer can become a part of my job instead of my pleasure. The reality is, when prayer becomes a duty, it totally misses what God had in mind. I suppose that's why the Lord, through the prophet Isaiah, had this to say:

"Even them will I bring to my holy mountain, and make them joyful in my house of prayer…" (Isaiah 56:7a)

And again, God speaking through the Psalmist, "You will show me the path of life: in Your presence is fullness of Joy; at Your right hand there are pleasures for evermore." (Psalm 16:11)

Though I still enjoy hooking and landing large fish, nowadays I find myself being more and more satisfied by simply spending quality time with Him. It is there, in His presence, that I'm able to offload all my burdens, receive His counsel and encouragement for the day, and above it all, just enjoy being with the most beautiful person in all of creation—God Himself.

I don't know about you, but I stand amazed. How He manages to carve out personal time for each person who's willing to meet with Him is beyond me. Yet, somehow, He does it. The wonder of that has me spending a lot more time with Him than I used to. The One who created and now sustains all things is not too busy to spend time with each of us. He's not racing to His next appointment. He's not thinking about other things He'd rather be doing; He just loves being with us. That's incredible! To not respond, for me, is no longer an option.

Like a marriage relationship that has gone from the beauty of desire to the drudgery of duty, if we are not careful, the same thing can happen with our relationship with God. Fortunately, if we are willing to return to Him, He is more than willing to meet us right where we are.

*"Delight thyself also in the LORD; and he shall give thee the desires of thine heart." (Psalm 37:4)*

# Taking God's Advice

It happened one day when I felt a need to encourage one of our children to slow down and reconsider some of the choices they had been making. Feeling a bit awkward because they are now an adult, I patiently waited for the right moment to present itself. In time, it did— at least that's what I thought.

"I'm in kind of a strange spot," I had told them, hoping to gain their undivided attention. "On one hand, I am so proud of you and want to do anything I possibly can to see you continue to grow and succeed in life. On the other hand, there are times when I see things that I know are going to cause you problems and I feel like I should say something. The trouble is, you're now an adult, and I would never want you to think that I'm trying to treat you like a kid."

I had hoped that my words would have revealed to them my heart and that they would have invited me to speak to them anytime I felt to do so. Unfortunately, that's not what happened. Though they were extremely polite and moved by my genuine care for them, they never did grant me a formal invitation to speak anytime I felt a need. So, our conversation ended as awkwardly as it had begun.

Later that day while working around the house, I was thinking about what had happened. It was then that it hit me. "Lord, have you ever seen things that I'm doing that You've wanted to talk to me about but I've not given You permission? Have I been polite to You but for whatever reason held You at a distance, perhaps afraid of what you might say?" The answers were plain. As I toggled between thoughts of how I felt for my own child and how God was feeling toward me, I melted. I have to tell you, that simple revelation has changed my life.

Nowadays, as a part of my daily prayer time, I intentionally stop, remember what happened that day, and invite God to speak to me about anything He wants. Because I know how I was feeling toward my own child, I also remember how He feels about me. He only wants to see me succeed and clearly, if anyone can do that, it's Him.

His desire for our success is greater than anyone else's. To shut Him out, and hold Him at bay, even if we are polite in doing so, is to miss out on the richest blessings life has to offer.

*(Proverbs 4:1-2) "Hear, you children, the instruction of a father, and attend to know understanding. For I give you good doctrine, forsake you not my law."*

# Dark Hoods and Feelings

The black hood slid over his head—an unnerving feeling to say the least. With no ability to see where he was going, my dad was in for a ride he would never forget. The man sitting beside him didn't make things any easier. Actually, he was determined to teach my dad a lesson.

As an officer and fighter pilot in the United States Air Force, my dad knew the job came with many dangers and risk. Having someone throw a black hood over his head is one he hadn't bargained for. Fortunately for him, when it happened he wasn't a prisoner of war but rather a flight student in instrument training school. As it is with so many of my dad's stories, this one immediately began speaking to me.

The classroom he was in was the cockpit of the TF102, the training version of the Delta Dagger fighter jet. It was there, while "flying under the hood" as they called it, that my dad learned one of life's most important lessons—you can't trust your feelings no matter how real they seem.

Here's how the lesson worked. With the instructor sitting at the student's side, and the black hood now covering his flight helmet, the student was given a series of maneuvers to perform with the aircraft. Turn left, descend, ascend, bank right then ultimately, level the plane out and fly straight. Once the instructor felt the student had adequate time to level the plane out, the hood came off and the student saw things the way they really were; usually in a turn and losing altitude. To hear my dad tell his story, it's clear the exercise forever changed the way he flew airplanes.

Though feelings have their place and of themselves are not evil, you just can't depend on them to keep you flying straight and on course. For the fighter pilot, who inevitably faces a rollercoaster of feelings while flying, learning to trust your instruments above your other senses is a matter of life and death. For the average person facing life's sharp turns and sudden drops, the same thing is true.

In the cockpit of life, I have found the Bible the most reliable instrument known to man. Though some like to debate its reliability, it nonetheless remains the most published and read book of all times. The reason: those who trust its guidance have found it to be true. For me, having flown with it and without it, it's a no-brainer. When I trust and practice what the Bible teaches, I do well. When I choose to make life decisions based on my feelings, I typically crash. I suppose that's why the scripture has this to say:

*"There is a way which seems right unto a man, but the end thereof are the ways of death."* (Proverbs 14:12) And again, *"Trust in the Lord with all your heart; and lean not unto your own understanding. In all your ways acknowledge Him, and He shall direct your paths."* (Proverbs 3:5-6)

Someone once said, "the Bible is truth; you either believe it or prove it. It is what it is." While I've never tried to fly an airplane with a hood over my head, God knows I've tried many other things that way. Thankfully, the lesson is finally sinking in. Though my eyes are open, and I'm free to look around, at the end of the day, my real confidence remains on the Word of God. It has never steered me wrong.

*"Your Word is a lamp unto my feet, and a light unto my path."*
*(Psalm 119:105)*

# Hand in Hand, Christ and His Church

As we stepped into the cool water, our pace all but stopped. My feet sore from wearing new sandals, the shallow slough was as refreshing as it gets. I grabbed my wife's hand, sighed deeply, and took a fresh breath of Amelia Island salt air. There are few things I enjoy more than holding my wife's hand and walking on the beach. On this particular day, when our feet hit the water and her hand hit mine, it was as if I was translated to another place; actually, to several.

From the darker sands of Indonesia, set with a backdrop of Christian persecution and bloodshed, to the swarming streets of Mumbai India; from communist Cuba, to war torn Africa, to the frigid Ukraine; from threatened Israel, to the streets of Rome, my wife has placed her hand in mine literally all over the world. I've pulled her up onto trains in the middle of the night not knowing the language or when it was our turn to get off. I've helped her up onto the backs of camels and then back down again. Through dark allies in the night visiting families living in condemned buildings, to the steps of double-decker buses in London, taking my wife's hand in marriage has meant more than either one of us imagined.

By her hand, I've helped her in and out of our boat, on to the dance floor, over puddles in the street, and on and on. And so it should be. The reason—from God's perspective marriage is a picture of Christ's love for His church, His bride. It's also a picture of her love for Him.

When I think of the way my dear wife has stood by my side through thick and thin, I am humbled. She has joyfully followed me into places that many would refuse to go. Her devotion and friendship has taught me more about what God is looking for in my life than anyone else I know.

All throughout the Bible there is a theme of Love. In order to make that message practical for us, God instituted marriage. From Adam and Eve being the perfect counter-parts for each other, to Jesus performing His first miracle at the wedding celebration in Cana of Galilee, God's love for marriage is far more significant than many realize. I suppose that's why the final chapters of the Bible are dedicated to it. I also think it's why the devil hates it so much.

At the great marriage supper of the Lamb, all true followers of Christ will have the privilege of being called His "bride" for all of eternity (Revelation 19:7-9). Notice I said "followers of Christ." It's one thing to say we *believe* in Jesus but another to *follow* Him where He leads us. That thought brings another scripture to mind—Revelation 14:4b "these are they who follow the Lamb wherever He goes..." Though I realize I may be stirring up some theological conflicts, the rule to keep things simple works well here.

God is love. To make that practical and understandable for us, He instituted this thing called marriage. When it's working correctly, it's a small picture of a much more fulfilling and eternal relationship. As Christ has loved us all to the point of laying down His life for us, so ought men to lay down their lives for their wives. In like fashion, when a woman feels such deep and genuine love from her husband, she is happy to follow him to the ends of the earth just as the church does with Jesus (Ephesians 5:22-32). For me, my wife's hand in mine is the gospel plain and simple.

*"Wives, submit yourselves unto your own husbands, as unto the Lord. For the husband is the head of the wife, even as Christ is the head of the church: and he is the savior of the body. Husbands, love your wives, even as Christ also loved the church, and gave himself for it." (Ephesians 5:22-25)*

# Seeing From God's Point of View

The colors exceeded my vocabulary; so deep, so dazzling—heavenly. As I watched, they changed. With ever increasing beauty, my sense of wonder turned to worship. Only God could make something so spectacular.

Of late, I've seen some gorgeous sunrises at the beach. On this day God out did Himself. As is my custom, though I'm usually there for prayer, if the scene calls for it, I get out my iPhone and snap a couple of pictures. Without question, this was one of those days. As I positioned my phone on the side mirror of my car to steady the shot, the scene suddenly changed. The timing couldn't have been worse.

To give the man the benefit of the doubt, he probably didn't know I was trying to take a picture. Back and forth he walked, with head down, pacing in some kind of aimless pattern that seemed stuck right in my line of sight. His presence was blocking one of the most gorgeous sunrises I think I've ever seen. Though at first I thought his pacing would eventually carry him out of the way and then I might get a picture, it just didn't happen. Now I know why.

The man's appearance was not an impressive one: cut-off sleeves, ragged pants, and perhaps homeless. Little did I know how God would use him to speak to me. In a moment when I was a little frustrated because he was standing in the way of my getting a picture of God's beautiful creation, God refocused my lens. "*He's* the thing that I think is most beautiful," the Lord seemed to be saying. Those words pierced my heart.

With camera poised and ready to shoot, I refocused my shot according to God's definition of beauty. Again and again, I took pictures of the man until finally he decided to walk away. The photos of him, with the gorgeous sunrise in the background, are now among my most favorite.

When I think about the incident, this passage comes to mind: "When I consider Your heavens, the work of Your fingers, the moon and the stars, which You have ordained; what is man that You are mindful of him? and the son of man, that You visit him?" (Psalms 8:3-

4). Also verse 6, "You made Him to have dominion over the works of Your hands; You have put all things under His feet."

Now I'm not sure how it is for you, but for me, the thought that God, the Creator of all things, considers us the crowning point of His creation is hard to conceive; especially when you throw in all our current issues. Nonetheless, it is how He sees us.

In hindsight, I wish I had had a chance to speak to the man. If I had, I wonder how he would have responded to God's view of him. The idea that God saw him as more beautiful than the explosive sunrise we had both just witnessed would likely have been hard for him to receive. Truth is, he's probably not alone. It never ceases to amaze me how many of us struggle with the fact that God loves us all so deeply. Though we often get things out of focus, He does not. His love for us is undeniable—issues and all. For me, that's a picture God wants us all to have.

*"From the rising of the sun unto the going down of the same the LORD's name is to be praised." (Psalm 113:3)*

# Fountains, Algae and Narrow Places

I had a pond dug in my front yard. In an effort to keep the algae down, along with my wife's comments, I added a small fountain. It really is quite nice. Not only is it aerating the few fish, and keeping the water moving, it's also pretty to look at. The added points I gained with the wife by installing it have been well worth the investment.

While standing and gazing at it one day, the mechanics of our new little fountain began speaking to me. It's beautiful flowering cone-like shape, shooting into the air then gracefully falling in a circular pattern, all occur because of two important things: power (the pump) and a tiny opening (the nozzle) that the water gets forced through.

Now few would argue that to get anything done in life, you have to have some power. Individuals want it. Churches want it. Businesses want it. Countries want it. Without question, power is essential to life and progress. Even Jesus gave it to His church to ensure her success. Tiny openings, on the other hand, like the nozzle on our fountain, are usually underrated—at least by us. As is the case with so many things, Jesus sees it differently.

"Because strait is the gate, and narrow is the way, which leads unto life, and few there be that find it." Those are Jesus' words found in Matthew 7:14. According to Him, narrow places are not optional but essential to our entering into the Kingdom of God. Though I don't claim to know all the reasons why, here are a few things that I've learned.

When passing through narrow difficult places, we have to examine the stuff we are carrying. Is it really that important? Do I really need it? Like the children of Israel wandering in the wilderness and having to set up and tear down the tabernacle every time God decided to move, I'm sure, in time, they only took the stuff they had to.

The other interesting thing about narrow places is that they serve as a test. I've found that most people like to identify with big and prosperous, but narrow and small -- not so much. Yet it is often in those tight places that God refines and tests a person's true resolve and motive. Like the 'camel having to pass through the eye of a needle,' letting go of stuff we count dear is not easy. If we are doing things for the right reasons, God is more than willing to help us make it through (Luke 18:25-27). In the end, life's tight places are well worth the squeeze if we just hang in there and let God have His way. Just ask Jesus. His cross gave way to His open grave and eternal life for all who believe.

Like our pretty fountain, just on the other side of life's narrow and tough places is something beautiful and worth having. Though we need the power of God to make it so, without the narrow places, we will never really reach our true height and potential. To me, a willingness to go through such places for Jesus' sake is the true test of what real Christianity is all about.

*"Humble yourselves therefore under the mighty hand of God, that He may exalt you in due time: Casting all your care upon Him because He cares for you." (1Peter 5:6)*

*"For it is easier for a camel to go through a needle's eye, than for a rich man to enter into the kingdom of God. And they that heard it said, Who then can be saved? And he said, The things which are impossible with men are possible with God." (Luke 18:25-27)*

# Pride, Galoshes and Cold Feet

"Here," Fernando, my father-in-law, said to Irene, my mother-in-law. "You're going to need these."

"What are they?" she asked with a puzzled look.

"They're galoshes," he said matter-of-factly. "You put them over your shoes. Where we are going, they are a must."

"I am not wearing those," she pushed back. "Those are ugly."

Fernando was a man of few words who said a ton through his silence. The day Irene refused to accept his gift, his lack of response was nothing new. The fact that they were newlyweds only further proved how wise, even in his youth, he really was.

By the time they arrived at their new home and Irene had opened her car door and buried her stylish shoe in ten inches of snow, Fernando's silence filled the atmosphere. The cold snow, now working its way around her Texas grown foot, made her draw back and rethink her position.

Now if you've ever met my mother-in-law, you know she's one of the most delightful, fun to be around people on the planet. Though not afraid to voice her opinion, she's also not afraid to admit her mistakes—especially after chilling in the snow for a little while. Her sheepish request, as to what her husband had done with the ugly rubber galoshes, is one I would have loved to have been there to hear. Though not quite the same, listening to her tell the story, is almost as fun.

When I think about my mother-in-law's resistance to put on something essential to where she was going, I can't help but think about myself. I must confess, like Irene, in my early years I was more concerned about looking good in front of people rather than paying attention to life's realities. Unfortunately, the same thing was true of me spiritually.

Even though I grew up going to church, the thought of putting on Jesus Christ publicly was something that I felt would cramp my style. The day I realized how cold life without God really was, all that changed. To finally humble myself and admit that I needed something that God had been offering to me took some time. Once I did admit it, I realized just how much my pride had been hurting me.

To me, without question, it's our biggest issue—pride. From Genesis to Revelation, it is the root of all our problems. From the moment Adam chose to be his own god instead of having the true God, everything went downhill. Some call that tragic event in the Garden of Eden the fall of man. I prefer calling it the rise of man. In essence, it was there that man said to God, "I don't need what you have to offer me; I'll do it my way." Like Fernando with Irene, God, in His infinite wisdom, decided not to argue the point but to let man step out into a world void of the protection He had offered him. The rest is history.

Fortunately, there is good news. Like my mother-in-law, if we are willing to humble ourselves and admit that we need God and His gracious gift, He is ever ready to help us out. As for me, galoshes or not, putting on Jesus Christ was the best decision I've ever made.

*"But put you on the Lord Jesus Christ, and make not provision for the flesh, to fulfil the lusts thereof." (Romans 13:14)*

# Israel, Islam and the Cross

His comments pulled me in. As a writer for the Jerusalem Post, listening to Ari brought some critical things into focus for me. Finally, someone who seemed to know. As a former soldier in the Israeli Defense Force and devout worshiper of the God of Abraham, Isaac, and Jacob, Ari's insights where dripping with things not heard on our news channels.

When possible, I love listening to those of differing views. If nothing else, it makes me stop and ponder why I believe the things I do. When it came to Ari, though deeply Jewish, his willingness to address a group of Christians gathered in someone's home touched me in ways I had not expected. According to him, he too left with things to ponder.

It started after he made an interesting comment about the philosophical differences between Judaism, Islam and Christianity. According to him, devout Jewish people tend to see Christianity as all about mercy and forgiveness. Conversely, when it comes to Islam, devout Jewish people tend to see Muslims viewing their God as being all about justice and harsh punishments for wrong doing. For the observant Jewish person, things are different. According to Ari, they see God as both Just and Merciful. To him, this is what sets Judaism apart from all the other religions of the world. For me, it's the very thing that links Christianity and Judaism together.

Here's how I respectfully explained it to Ari. "For the Christian, Jesus dying on the cross is the ultimate act of both God's Justice and His Mercy. Justice in that a crime had been committed—our sin—and it needed to be paid for with an appropriate consequence. That's why Jesus had to die. On the issue of mercy, the fact that God laid the punishment that belonged to us on Him and then extended forgiveness to all who believe, to me that's mercy at its best. Throw on top of that the resurrection of Jesus from the dead, and all the pieces come together.

"According to both Jewish and Christian scriptures, death came into the world as a result of Adam and Eve's sin. For the Christian, the idea of God raising Jesus from the dead makes perfect sense. If death came into the world as a result of sin, then it's only fitting that life from the dead would be the result of payment for sin. In essence, the resurrection of Jesus Christ is God's way of demonstrating that Justice is settled and His Mercy is available to all who repent and believe. In the end, God is both extremely just and extremely merciful."

Ari's response was measured and sincere. "I've never heard it put quite that way."

Though neither one of us converted to the others total view of things, the fact that we were able to freely share our hearts, with no strings attached, was no doubt pleasing to the Lord. The insights I gained from him and his zeal for God, have stuck with me until this day. I pray the same thing is true for him.

*"Surely He has borne our griefs, and carried our sorrows: yet we did esteem Him stricken, smitten of God, and afflicted. But He was wounded for our transgressions, He was bruised for our iniquities: the chastisement of our peace was upon Him; and with His stripes we are healed." (Isaiah 53:4-5)*

# Eating Custard and Truth

"That was a great meal!" I told my soon-to-be wife as she rose from the table and made her way toward the kitchen.

"Thanks!" she said, "Would you like some coffee and dessert?"

"Sure," I replied. "Do you need some help?"

"No, I've got it," she said. "Just relax and I'll be right back."

"Wow!" I remember thinking, "This is wonderful! God has really blessed me. Not only has He brought me a wonderful person to be my wife, she's a great cook too!" As I sat thinking about all the great things God had done for me and the love I felt towards both Him and my fiancé, in she walked carrying her famous dessert.

"What is it?" I asked.

"Pujim," she said with an obvious air of pride. "It's a Brazilian custard," she continued, as she placed it on the table absolutely sure I was going to love it.

"Oh great!" I said, as I stared at the perfectly browned coconut topping that covered the dish fit for a magazine. As she made her way back to the kitchen to get the coffee and some plates, I continued starring at the dessert. Now I realize that some people love things like coconut and custards, but I'm not one of them. Don't ask me why, but just the thought makes me want to shudder. As my bride-to-be made her way back to the table, anxious for me to try her famous Pujim, I was gearing up to eat, for love's sake, what I absolutely hated.

"Just a small piece," I said in an attempt to minimize the trauma while trying not to hurt her feelings. And with that, she cut a piece that to me was the size of Texas. Bite by bite I worked my way through until finally I finished.

"Well, what did you think?" she asked as I drank my coffee trying to drown the taste.

"Oh, it was good," I said in a voice that lacked conviction. "As far as custards go with coconut," I continued in my thoughts only. Now I know I wasn't altogether truthful, and I've since gotten things straight with God and her, but I just couldn't bring myself to hurt her feelings. It wasn't until after we were married that I told how I felt about her Pujim with coconut. To my surprise, she wasn't hurt at all, but rather wanted to know what I did like.

"Chocolate!" was my emphatic answer. "I like chocolate." With that, at least for me, our married life went to a whole new level.

It's been my experience that many times we go through life thinking we're pleasing the Lord, but wonder why He's not responding. I can assure you, it's not because He doesn't love us. Nothing could be farther from the truth. What I've found is that while we can know *about* God, we need to know Him personally, His likes and dislikes.

Like in the early stages of any relationship, there's always a lot of learning to do. If we persist, eventually love and good communication will give way to a life filled with all the pleasures God intends for each one of us to have. I've tried a lot of things in life, but I can honestly say that knowing and being known by God is by far the greatest of them all.

*"But if any man love God, the same is known of him." (1 Corinthians 8:3)*

# Tool Boxes and Padlocks

For Mike, the lock hanging on his tool box wasn't funny. Who would dare play such a prank? He was the foreman. For him, one thing was clear—it wouldn't happen again. Looking back, that lock changed Mike's life forever.

I'm all ears when people start telling me their stories. The fact is, through other people's stories God is often speaking to me. With Mike's story, nothing could be truer.

At a machine shop, a man's tools are his pride. For Mike, who had worked his way up to shop foreman, his tools had become his enemy. It seemed that every time one of the machinists working under Mike had a problem, Mike always had an answer. The answer was located in his tool box. He had every tool a man could ever want. Not only that, he knew just how to use it to get the job done.

Sadly, that was Mike's problem. The day his boss, the owner of the company, threw a padlock on Mike's toolbox, was the day Mike's world took a big turn; if it hadn't, he might have been looking for another job.

To hear Mike tell the story, and to hear how grateful he now is for his boss's tough response to his problem, brings some important things into view. If you haven't figured out *why* Mike's willingness to roll up his sleeves, break out his tools and help those under him get the job done was wrong, let me explain. Mike's job was to manage the crew—not to turn wrenches. Every time he would pull out his tools and get rolled up in someone else's job, he was no longer able to fulfill his own. In the end, what seemed like a noble thing was hindering the business's success.

As a leader who has struggled with the same tendency, Mike's story has been a great reminder. When I read about the first century church and how the Holy Spirit organized their first missionary journey, I'm further convinced that Mike's boss knew just what he was doing. You can read the church's story in the book of Acts 13:2. As certain leaders had assembled and were seeking God together, this is what the

Holy Spirit said to them: "Separate me Barnabas and Saul for the work whereunto I have called them." Without going too deep, the word separate in the Greek language means "to limit." That's right, God was saying, I don't want these guys spread out too thin. For the mission to succeed, you have to limit them to what I've called them to do.

As someone who's seen both ditches on either side of the road, staying in your assigned place and doing it well, is not as easy as one might think—especially if you're the kind of person who likes to be in the thick of all the action.

We've each received a special grace and calling from God. Though it's true that there are seasons when we need to spin several plates in order to get things done, it's never a good long-range plan. To be effective and to be healthy, we all need to limit ourselves to the main assignment we've received. To not do so could earn us an unexpected padlock from the boss.

*"But we will not boast of things without our measure, but according to the measure of the rule which God has distributed to us, a measure to reach even unto you." (2 Corinthians 10:13)*

# Lessons On Liver

The quivering mound of liver lay naked on the table. For my wife, it had become a common sight. Usually wrapped in some kind of brown paper, the routine delivery was something she had learned to live with. Yuk! *Liver!* Just the thought makes me shudder. Over the course of her childhood, my wife actually learned to like it. Not me. While it's true that we grew up in very different parts of the world, none of that matters. As I see it, liver is liver.

Of all the memories my wife has shared of growing up in South America, Mr. Fell's routine delivery of quivering mounds of liver is the one I identify with most. At the time, she was living in Punta Arenas, the southernmost tip of Chile. Mr. Fell was a nearby rancher who had become a close family friend. The mounds of beef liver, well, let's just say they were his way of keeping the family friendship alive. Unfortunately, not everyone was happy about it. Take for instance my wife's childhood friend Patty. Just the thought of eating liver was enough to make her gag. If it hadn't been for my wife's mom Irene, Patty would have been just fine. Here's why.

Every time Mr. Fell would make his delivery of freshly harvested liver, Irene would be sure to share some with all her neighbors. For Patty that was terrible news. On one particular day, when Mr. Fell first started making his deliveries, Patty slipped out of her house to see if she could have lunch with my wife's family. When she told them why, Irene said, "Honey, you're more than welcome to have lunch with us today, but we're having liver too." According to my wife and her mother, the pitiful look on Patty's face said it all—she might as well just go back home.

When I think about the story and my wife's childhood friend, Patty, Jesus' words to His disciples come to mind. "And into whatsoever house you enter, first say, Peace be to this house. And if the Son of peace be there, your peace shall rest upon it: if not, it shall turn to you again. And in the same house remain, eating and drinking such things as they give: for the laborer is worthy of his hire. Go not from house to house.

And into whatsoever city you enter, and they receive you, eat such things as are set before you:" (Luke 10:5-8)

Let's face it, not everything we get served is what we like. Just the same, if we are in the place of God's choosing, the place marked by His peace, then what is served is usually just what we need—like it or not. Ok, so let me throw a little liver on the table right here. As a pastor, I'm amazed as I watch how many Christian disciples go from house to house, or can I say church to church, because something is served that they don't like. Not that there are not legitimate times of transition, but more often than not, it seems to me that Jesus' words are being ignored. Though by no means am I the judge of such things—just an observer— I have seen the benefits for those who tough it out and stay true to the place God has called them to.

As hard as that may be at times, in the end, I'm convinced those who swallow hard and say amen will have the goods to reveal the true Love of God to a world that's in desperate need.

*"Now no chastening for the present seemeth to be joyous, but grievous: nevertheless afterward it yieldeth the peaceable fruit of righteousness unto them which are exercised thereby." (Hebrews 12:11)*

# Revival, Vietnam and Healing Hearts

With each step, Alan pushed back his fear. Dead and wounded soldiers lie scattered on the jungle floor. The groans and cries of his wounded comrades were strangely louder than the explosions just over the hill. The earth shook and so did he. Nearby, the drone sound of helicopter blades, awaiting his return, offered the only hope he had. If he could only recover one more soldier, it would still be worth it all. It was there, while lifting his leather boot and stepping over another slain body that it happened. Alan froze in his place.

Years ago, I was in a series of revival meetings held in our church. Though various Christian movements and traditions define such gatherings differently, generally speaking, they are meetings set aside as an invitation to the Holy Spirit to come and to save and revive people. On the night that Alan had his Vietnam flashback, without question, the Holy Spirit had accepted our invitation to come and minister to those in need.

To know Alan, at a glance, you would never guess he had been through so much. A quiet guy with a servant's heart, for years even his wife didn't know about the prestigious medals he had received for his service to our country. As a helicopter pilot, shot down more than once, his job was the recovery of the dead and wounded. The night the memories came flooding back, little did he know how God was getting ready to rescue him.

I should tell you, I pastor a charismatic church. "Charismatic" is a term used to describe an acceptance of the grace gifts given by the Holy Spirit as relevant and for today. Though not embraced by all, since the beginning of the 1960s, what has been called the Charismatic movement has swept over the entire world and transformed millions of Protestants and Catholics alike.

The reason I share that is not to foster debate but because of what happened to Alan. You see, historically one of the manifestations experienced in Charismatic churches is something called being "slain in the Spirit." In short, it's what happens when someone experiences the presence of God in such an overwhelming way that they can no longer remain standing. Like the priest in the Old Testament, prostrate on the floor because the glory of God had filled the temple, such has been the experience of multitudes since that time (2 Chronicles 5:13-14)

On the night Alan received an inner healing, interestingly, he got touched not while lying on the floor but while stepping over someone who was. Remember I told you Alan had a servant's heart? Well, that's what God used to touch him. While stepping over someone to help someone else, Alan had a flashback of Vietnam. It was then that the Lord spoke to him. "These here are not the dead, but the living." And with that, the Lord reached down and pulled out all the hurt, all the trauma and all the grief. To this day, Alan's never been the same.

Personally, I like it when God shows up in unexpected ways. Though by no means every spiritual manifestation is from the Lord, I thank God for the ones that are. With the Scriptures and the Holy Spirit as our guide, there's no doubt in my mind that, across denominational lines, God is touching lives in unprecedented and sometimes unusual ways. As for me, I continue to invite Him to come and to revive us all.

*"And it shall come to pass in the last days, says God, I will pour out of my Spirit upon all flesh..."* *(Acts 2:17a)*

# Three Year Olds and God's Love

"Hold me Papa." His voice pulled hard on my heart. "Hold me tight," he said again. This time he nestled his head against my chest. I pulled him close and squeezed as hard as I felt a three-year-old could stand.

Recently, I helped my grandson overcome some childhood fears. With his whole world seeming a bit upside down and Mimi and I temporarily taking care of him, I knew in order to help him, I needed to get his mind focused on good things to come.

"We're going to get on an airplane," I told him, "and fly way up in the sky."

"We are?" he said looking up with one eye a little more open than the other.

"Yep," I told him. "And it's going to be a ton of fun."

"When Papa? Are we going now?" he said hoping to see his Dad soon.

"Not now but in a couple of days," I said. My voice was as convincing as I knew how to make it. Unfortunately, two days seemed like forever to him. Slowly his fears and insecurities crawled back up onto the blue leather recliner where we were sitting.

That's when I had the idea—a picture. "Do you want to see the airplane?" I asked as I grabbed my laptop and pulled it up on to our laps. Suddenly his interest returned. Picture after picture, plane after plane, inside and out, I explained to him, over and over, just how things would be. I told him how we would have to buckle our seat belts and how the captain's voice would come on—I left nothing out. The result was amazing. Though I had to keep the vision alive for the full two days, it, coupled with periodic big squeezes, kept his head above water.

I even went as far as taking him to the airport the night before our departure. We walked on the moving sidewalk and we saw where we would check our bags. We watched people going through the security check and did everything I could think of to pass the time and settle his heart.

Up to then, for him, everything had hinged on my words and a few pictures on the computer. He simply had to trust me. Once we physically went to the airport that changed. My words were real. He knew that all that I had said was actually going to happen. You can only imagine how excited he was the next morning. I must say, he was three years old the entire trip.

After safely handing him off to his dad, the Lord began speaking to me. Though far from three years old, I know what it's like to need God to still my storms and to help me regain my focus in life. Without a doubt, at some level, the way the Lord led me to encourage my grandson is the way He loves and cares for us all.

Like my grandson, there are times when we just need God to hold us and hold us tight. There are moments when having to wait two days seems like forever and when we need God to pull fresh vision for our future up onto our lap. I think above everything, the fact that I was committed to personally make the trip with my grandson is what gave him the most peace. For me, it's the thing I love most about God as well.

*"Sing, O heavens; and be joyful, O earth; and break forth into singing, O mountains: for the LORD hath comforted his people, and will have mercy upon his afflicted." (Isaiah 49:13)*

# Trains, Wrecks and Miracles

Light exploded through the driver side window. Like the sun in all its strength—so bright, so powerful. For an instant, he froze. Then it hit. The engineer cringed as his train crushed and plowed my friend's small white car down the tracks.

For the engineer, stopping was pointless. In his mind, the driver was most certainly dead. As he radioed the train station to report the incident, he told them there was no need to hurry. No one could have possibly survived. For my friend, who was very much still alive, life would never be the same. Thrown from his car which ultimately landed back on top of him, he lay trapped in the very dent the train had created when it hit. There, conscious and alone, the dark African night offered him no comfort.

Rhodesia (modern day Zimbabwe) at that time was in utter chaos. Civil war and brutal conflict occupied every border but one—South Africa, where many fled. For my friend and his family, they had decided to stay in order to offer whatever help they could. Ironically, that's what he was doing the night the train hit him.

Though the place where it happened was extremely rural, in Africa it's quite common for people to show up out of seemingly nowhere. Such was the case with my friend. From the bush, African voices began filling the air around the car where he was pinned. Unfortunately, they too had decided that no one could have survived such a crash. As they proceeded to take everything they could find, namely all the supplies he was carrying to a group of local pastors, my friend's pain and despair grew. Trapped and listening, there was nothing he could do. When they finally left, the silence was greater than that left behind by the roaring train.

I don't know about you, but I find stories of miraculous interventions fascinating. If you saw the pictures of my friend's little white car, the dent where he was allowed to lie, and the good health he possesses today, I'm sure you would agree. Miracles still happen! When I consider the thousands of pastors all over the world he's ministered to since that time, I'm equally amazed. Not only did God miraculously spare his life, but ultimately turned tragedy into blessing.

For my friend, the supplies he was carrying, things like, bread, jam, tea, etc. were lost. Though he was unable to hand them out to the group of pastors that night, what he's been able to hand out since that time has been far greater. The testimony of God's faithfulness in the most difficult of situations has made my friend, Dr. David Wynns, one of the greatest encouragers I know. And to think, in part, he received his current grace in the midst of a terrible situation.

While it's not true of all, for some, you feel like you've just been mowed over by a train. If that's not you, you likely know someone to whom the statement fits. Regardless, I'm writing to remind us all of God's amazing ability to turn horrible situations around for our good.

While at the moment you may feel pinned underneath things and written off by those around you, real help is on the way. God's not done with you who trust and believe.

*"Fear you not; for I am with you: be not dismayed; for I am your God: I will strengthen you; yes, I will help you; I will uphold you with the right hand of my righteousness." (Isaiah 41:10)*

# Moms, Memories and Love

Of all the people walking toward me, seeing her brought my world to a stop. Who would have thought? Waist deep in cool water, unexpected tears began to fill my eyes. I stretched out my hand and helped her in. As I did, a host of childhood memories eased into the water with her.

My mom—there's no one like her. Years ago, I had the privilege of having her with me as my wife and I led a group of worshipers to the Holy Land. It's an experience I'll cherish forever. When we got to the Jordan River, the place where John the Baptist baptized Jesus, I had no idea how having my mom present was going to hit me. Even though I knew I would be baptizing people in the Jordan, and that my mom was likely one of those people, seeing her walk down the steps and into the water is something I really wasn't ready for.

A wave of gratitude for all she'd ever done for me made my role as pastor/son hard to figure out. Just the same, it was one of the most beautiful moments of my life. The fact that she was there for me when I was born and now, I was able to be there for her as she publicly confessed being born again, was no small privilege.

From the womb forward, I'm sure you would agree moms are God's gift to us all. As the one who not only births us, but, by and large, sticks with us no matter what, they are a great picture of God's unconditional love. In the home I grew up in, the examples are endless. From skinned knees, to broken bones, to caring for us while my dad was in Vietnam, to homework, to meal prep, to bee stings, to laundry, to sibling squabbles and on and on, my mom has been there through it all. Though she's clearly human, such love could only be divine.

On the day I baptized my mom in the Jordan River, that same kind of love, the love of Christ, overshadowed us both. As my mom came up out of the water and we hugged, eternal life joined us in the embrace. No, the clouds didn't part and God didn't audibly speak from heaven like He did for those watching Jesus on the day He was baptized, but He didn't need to. The love we felt said it all.

When we take time to honor our mothers, I want to personally say thanks to God for mine. Not only has she loved me through some really tough stuff, but by doing so she's given me a taste of who God really is. Thanks mom. God's persistent love and encouragement through you has marked me forever.

*"Her children arise up, and call her blessed; her husband also, and he praises her. Many daughters have done virtuously, but you excel them all." (Proverbs 31:28-29)*

# Koi Fish, Patience and Hope

Koi fish—in Japan and China, they're a symbol of strength. At my house, they've come to mean something else. Ever since I dug a pond in my front yard, I've had one interesting experience after another. When I decided to add some colorful Koi fish, I was clueless as to what I was in for.

It started when my neighbor told me I could have the two huge ones that were swimming in his pond. When I say huge, they were at least 30 inches long and well fed. That sounded great until I tried to move them. The thought of an easy transfer swam away as quickly as they did. I had no idea they could move so fast. I tried cast-netting them, seine netting them, and I even went as far as to build a trap. Nothing worked. So, I moved to plan B—grow my own.

Actually, it was another neighbor's idea. Though the ones she bought me were only 3 inches long, she offered to raise them in her tank until they would be safe to release in my pond. The few largemouth bass I have would easily gobble them up being so small. I must say that waiting for those little Koi to grow was painfully slow. Truth is, the day my 3-year-old grandson and I released them in our pond, their size was questionable. The fact that they disappeared and I didn't see them again spoke for itself.

Determined to not be defeated, I came up with a different approach. I bought a large plastic storage bin, drilled some holes in it, put a brick inside, bought some new Koi, daily fed them, and put the lid on to keep the birds out. Unfortunately, I hadn't thought about the raccoons. No joke, they popped the lid at night and got them both. After one other attempt, that I won't even try to explain, I finally decided to just let it go and focus on more important stuff.

Shortly after that is when it happened. While walking around the pond one day, I saw him—a beautiful Koi fish about 13 inches long. I was in shock. Two days later, I saw the second one. A good six months had passed since my grandson and I had released the two small Koi that my neighbor had grown. Because I hadn't seen them, and because the bass looked really happy, the conclusion seemed obvious. Boy was I wrong.

The entire time I was feeling like I was losing the battle, God was growing things in the dark murky places just beyond my view. The day they suddenly appeared, the Lord seized the moment to talk to me. "Your labors are not in vain," He said. "I've been working in the secret places of your life, and in time, you're going to see what I've been doing and greatly rejoice." Immediately this scripture came to mind. I hope it speaks to you like it did to me:

*"Cast not away therefore your confidence, which hath great recompence of reward. For you have need of patience, that, after you have done the will of God, you might receive the promise. For yet a little while, and he that shall come will come, and will not tarry. Now the just shall live by faith: but if any man draw back, my soul shall have no pleasure in him." (Hebrews 10:35-38)*

# Airports, Stickers and Speaking Up

Moments of inspiration are easy to miss, especially when they sneak up from behind you. It almost happened to me at the airport in London. There, while standing in line at a Starbucks, a man eased up from behind me and began speaking to me in a cautious whisper. "You don't need to look back," he said, "but you have a large sticker on the back of your pants, evidently from the store where you recently bought them." As I turned to see who was talking to me, and then slid my hand back to confirm what he had said, I had to chuckle—in a whisper of course—as I discretely pealed the five-inch-long sticker off and then thanked him for telling me.

The thought of walking around with that sticker on my backside for most of the day was both humbling and funny—once I got over myself. While sipping my coffee and thinking more about it, I couldn't help but consider all the other people who had seen it but didn't have the courage to let me know. It was then that inspiration pulled up a chair beside me and began to speak.

Why are we afraid to help each other with things that everyone knows need fixing? Though I may be wrong, my guess is that the man who was kind enough to tell me probably had worn his own stickers around too. Having felt the embarrassment of such moments, he, no doubt, felt compelled to help me out.

While he was heading to India and I to Africa, our brief interaction reminded me of a simple but powerful truth. We are our brother's keeper. If for some reason you are not familiar with that phrase, its origin is the Bible. The account I'm referring to is found in the book of Genesis chapter four. In it, two brothers, Cain and Abel, bring separate offerings to the Lord. One of the offerings God accepts and the other He refuses. Because Cain's offering was unacceptable, he became jealous and killed his brother. When God asked him where His brother was, Cain's reply was simply, "I know not: am I my brother's keeper?" (Genesis 4:9) Though God does not answer that question directly, His response makes it clear. Yes, we all are our brother's keeper.

Without question, we all have blind spots. To not do what we can to help cover each other's backs is to miss the second most important commandment in the Bible.

*"Jesus said unto him, you shalt love the Lord thy God with all your heart, and with all your soul, and with all your mind. This is the first and great commandment. And the second is like unto it, you shalt love your neighbour as yourself." (Matthew 22:37-39)*

# Tour Guides and Staying Close

At first, the intermittent radio signal didn't bother me. There was too much else going on. As I paused to take it all in, I found myself a prisoner to my surroundings. Beyond me, my wife was lost in Italy's rich architecture and history. With thousands of people wandering around in dreamlike awe, our tour guide did her best to keep us all together.

Looking back, our earpiece radios were more important than either of us had realized. Not only were they our source of information as we stood in front of each new site, they kept us from getting lost in a chaotic sea of tourists. On the day our tour guide's voice disappeared, that lesson was forever etched into our hearts.

Italy. Of all the places in the world, when it comes to sightseeing, it's one of the richest. Though our travels abroad have always centered on missions work, our trip to Italy was pure pleasure—except when we got lost, that is. Late in the day and clueless as to where our bus was, the feeling of being totally disconnected from our group was sickening to say the least. And to think, it all started with a radio signal that had begun to fade in and out.

Now to place blame where blame belongs, we had been told to stay close to our guide. Our problem was, she often moved while we were still feasting on the previous site. Besides, as long as we could hear her in our earpiece, figuring out where she was, was easy enough. Unfortunately, when her voice began coming and going due to our getting out of range, we didn't move quickly enough to find her. The result was an unpleasant season that was no one's fault but our own. While no doubt multitudes of other tourists have experienced the same dilemma, I'm confident it's not just a tourist thing. It's a life thing.

I can't tell you how many times I've gotten disconnected from the Lord's voice because I allowed myself to get out of range. Distracted by other things, even good things, if not careful, any of us can find ourselves questioning where He is. For me, there's nothing worse. Thankfully, once we figure out that the reason for the disconnect is not His doing but ours and we've had a few moments to experience the pain of separation, things can begin to turn back around. That's if we'll pay better attention of course.

It's exactly what happened to the Shulamite woman in the book of The Song of Solomon found in the Bible. In Chapter 2 she is enjoying a wonderful interaction with her future bridegroom king. There, He tells her that the winter has past and that the spring time has come. Good things are happening and He wants to enjoy them together with her. He then invites her to follow Him out into a new and exciting season of life. Her response, though polite, is that He should go. She has decided to stay where she is. In the very next chapter 3 verse 1, she cannot find Him. The reason—when He moved, she didn't.

The good news is that after a desperate search, she finds Him again. When she does, she clings to Him and won't let Him go. Be assured, that's exactly what my wife and I did when we finally found our tour guide.

*"It was but a little that I passed from them, but I found Him whom my soul loves: I held Him, and would not let Him go…" (Song of Solomon 3:4a)*

# Hanging On In The Tough

In my mind, the sound was different from what other people heard. To them, I was riding a worn-out 1975 Honda motorcycle that needed engine work. To me, the sound was much better. I had learned to hear it in spite of how things really were. Ringing in my helmet, my motorcycle sounded as impressive as all the other bikes in the race.

As a kid, I loved motorcycles—especially dirt bikes. The only problem was I couldn't afford a nice one. Somehow delivering newspapers and cutting grass never put me in the same class as my rather- affluent neighbors. It was years before I could even buy one of their left-over, worn-out ones. Just the same, the one I did have served me better than I realized. Watching my friends come whizzing by me in a cloud of dirt was never fun. Eventually my lack of good equipment turned into an unexpected blessing.

I'll never forget the day when Kenny Smith, one of my neighborhood motocross heroes, stood on the sideline, cheering me on with two thumbs up as I plowed through a corner and passed by a group of other riders. Even I was in shock. The fact that I was still on my clunker and they were riding much newer and more powerful motorcycles made my transformation all the more impressive. It wasn't until years later that I figured out how the change occurred. The insight continues to speak to me even now.

Learning to ride my poor-handling clunker to the best my ability had actually driven my skill level to a whole new place. That's right - having to hang on to that heavy, poor handling, awkward motorcycle eventually made me a really good rider. While all the other guys were riding with their cushy suspension and powerful engines, I was wrestling for dear life just to keep from crashing. In the end, I got stronger and more skilled. By the time I actually was able to purchase a nicer, more competitive motorcycle, the difference was amazing. Without question, having to make do with little made me better in the end.

By now, I trust you see the application. In so many places and in so many ways, being forced to put up with things we wish were different ultimately; if we hang in there, we will draw out our real potential. I can't tell you how many times I've looked back and thanked God for the way tough situations have worked great things into my life. Though it usually isn't much fun while you're going through it, real change is right around the corner. Our job is to just hang on. Like the boy in the movie "The Karate Kid," little did he know how all the seemingly bad stuff he had to endure was actually preparing him for greatness. I'm convinced the same thing is true with us.

In the Psalms King David said it well when he confessed, "You have enlarged me when I was in distress." (Psalm 4:1) The apostle Paul, speaking out of his own experience, echoed the same thing. "And not only so, but we glory in tribulations also: knowing that tribulation worketh patience; And patience, experience; and experience, hope: And hope makes not ashamed; because the love of God is shed abroad in our hearts by the Holy Ghost which is given unto us." (Romans 5:3-5)

If it's true that learning to ride difficult things can actually make us better, then perhaps some of the stuff we face is not our enemy but our friend. For me it's absolutely been the case.

*"It is good for me that I have been afflicted; that I might learn your statutes." (Psalm 119:71)*

# Peace at Closed Doors

He straightened his leg and pressed the pedal to the floor. Nothing. My brother was about to crash and he knew it. The van's brakes had totally given out. Thankfully, he wasn't going that fast. Though normally speaking, having the remote-controlled chain-link gate not open when he pushed the button would have been an aggravation; this time it was a blessing in disguise. Fortunately, the owner of the gate agreed.

Years ago my two brothers lived in downtown Jacksonville. My older brother Rick had moved there to help my younger brother Scott as he was finishing up some important schooling. Because Scott has some physical challenges, Rick's job was to drive the van and help prepare meals. The day they were leaving the gated parking lot and the gate wouldn't open is a day that neither one of them will soon forget. Afterwards, when considering what might have happened if the gate had opened and they had been on the highway when the brakes had failed, they both agreed—things could have ended a lot worse.

Gates and doors that refuse to open are not always a bad thing. Sometimes, Life's closed doors are God's protection keeping us from things we've not yet understood. I can't tell you how many times I've been frustrated by it; nonetheless it's true. Closed doors are often our friend and not our enemy. Having crashed into a few of them myself, looking back and realizing what I didn't see then, I'm grateful that God kept them closed. Without question, when we've committed our lives into the Lord's hands, closed doors are just as important as opened ones. Unfortunately, when we are facing one, we don't always see it that way.

Balaam beat his donkey because he wouldn't let him move forward when he wanted to, although the donkey was protecting him from unseen danger. The apostles were forbidden to go into Asia because of something else God had in mind. Learning to not be frustrated when doors are closed is an essential quality we all should seek. (Numbers 22:21-35; Acts 16:6-10)

The good news is that although closed doors may keep us from moving when and where we want, they never stop God. He's always able to meet us right where we are. A great example of that is in John 20:19-23. With the doors locked, and the disciples huddled in fear, Jesus decided to enter the room anyway. I love that about the Lord. He's never limited by the stuff that limits us. In the case of the disciples, Jesus saw their closed door as an opportunity to cast His vision for their future. It was a far better vision than the one they currently found themselves embracing.

If I've surrendered my life to the Lord and the door I've been pushing on refuses to open, there's a good chance God's trying to show me something I've not yet considered. Like my two brothers, who later thanked God for keeping the gate closed, whether life's doors open or stay shut, I've learned to trust Him and be at peace realizing He knows best.

*"Then the same day at evening, being the first day of the week, when the doors were shut where the disciples were assembled for fear of the Jews, came Jesus and stood in the midst, and said unto them, Peace be unto you." (John 20:19)*

# Running, Hiding, and God's Mercy

When I saw him, I felt the pull. I don't know why, but it always seems to happen to me when I'm heading somewhere important. As I drove past him, he made his way off the shoulder of the road and down the embankment into the woods. That's when the Lord spoke to me. "I want you to turn around and offer him a ride."

"He went into the woods," I told the Lord, as if He hadn't noticed. I suppose I was hoping He'd let me off the hook. It didn't work. In my heart I knew what He wanted me to do. With a bit of reluctance, I made a U-turn and headed back. To my surprise, just as I pulled up to the spot, he emerged from the dense roadside vegetation.

About 15 or 16 years old, it was clear he was having a tough time. Startled by my sudden appearance, it took him a moment to respond to my offer to give him a lift. Once he did, we both were in for a surprise. I kid you not, he looked *just* like me! The same blue eyes, the same curly hair, even the dimple on the chin. At his age, I could have been his twin.

As he tucked his duffle bag between his legs and closed the door, I felt the presence of God come in the car with him. "My name's Rob. What's yours?" I said, bracing myself in the event his name was Rob too.

"Steve," he said.

"Where are you headed?" I asked.

"Can you take me to the police station?" he said. "I need to turn myself in."

"Sure," I said, trying to not to seem too nosey.

As he told me his story, I did my best to just listen. "I ran away from a program my parents put me in, in south Florida," he said. "Actually, my dad and stepmom put me there. My parents are divorced."

The pain in his voice was obvious. For days he had been running, hitchhiking and living in the woods. At the moment I had driven by, he had just reached the end of himself.

When it seemed right, I decided to share my story with him. I told how I had moved to Florida as an aimless 19-year-old, how the Lord had met me in all of my troubles, and how it was Him that had nudged me to turn my car around to pick him up that day. As I spoke, he listened. As I looked at him, I kept seeing myself. The resemblance was uncanny. By the time we reached the police station, he too was sensing the divine nature of our encounter.

After giving him my cell phone number and asking if I would mind if I prayed for him, he thanked me for the ride and the prayer and made his way to the front door of the police station. As he did, I had an overwhelming sense that he was going to be all right. How you might ask? Because the same God that had met me, had met him. There was no doubt in my mind that God's hand was on him.

That day the Lord challenged me. In all my racing around to accomplish my so called "important stuff," I had almost missed the very thing that mattered most—a person whom God was reaching out to. The fact that he looked just like me was an added bonus. Through my simple act of reluctant obedience, God had used him to remind me of the great grace that I had received so many years ago.

*"Blessed are the merciful for they shall obtain mercy." (Matthew 5:7)*

# Waiting for Special Words

There they sat, waiting for the door to open. Soldiers and proud of it. For my dad, these guys had become unexpected friends. All from different walks of life and various parts of the country, each of them had paid a great price to be where they were. For them, having to wait for the go ahead from those in charge was nothing new. Doing it from a wheelchair was.

Bingo. Yep, bingo. I never imagined my dad, a colonel and fighter pilot in the United States Air Force would even give it a second thought. On the day I unexpectedly popped in to see him at the V.A hospital in Lake City, bingo is where he was. Well, kind of. He and a group of other veterans were waiting in their wheelchairs to get into the auditorium. Side-by-side in two neat rows, they filled the hallway. I couldn't help but think of a group of fighter pilots getting ready to scramble their jets in order to defend our country. Though none of them were sitting as erect as they used to, all of them still carried the spirit of honor granted to those who serve.

Finding my dad in the line-up was easy. His black ball cap with a picture of the F-4 phantom (the last plane he flew) goes with him everywhere he does. By the time I made it past all the other wheelchairs and reached him, I felt several eyes following me. "Hey, dad!" I said, realizing I had come up on his bad side and that it would take him a minute to turn his head to see who it was. The smile that lit his face made the long drive worth every minute.

As we talked, all the other veterans gradually resumed their conversations—until I got ready to say goodbye that is. As I leaned over and hugged my dad and told him I loved him, the hallway went silent. At first I felt a little awkward. Once I realized what was happening, I decided to just continue. "I sure do appreciate you dad," I said. "I'll see you again soon, ok?"

"Ok," he said. "Love you too, son. Thanks for coming by."

And with that I did what I've had to do multiple times before: suck in my gut, push down my emotions and walk away. As I did, my eyes met the eyes of several other veterans sitting completely silent and watching me. Some turned their eyes away as if feeling embarrassed for having eavesdropped on a special moment with my dad. Others smiled gently and stared straight ahead as I passed by. For me, I found myself wanting to say to all of them the same words that I had said to my dad. They certainly all deserved and needed to hear them. Their moment of silence felt like they were honoring me as I had honored my dad.

I realized later, by their response, just how important the hug and the simple words I had spoken to my dad really were. "I love you and appreciate you" are words that no human being should have to go without.

It's always a perfect time to slow things down and say to one another those powerful words: "I love you and appreciate you." You never know who may be listening.

*"Love never fails…" (1Cor.13:8)*

# A Simple Count

"Ready?" I asked. "One, two, three!"

"No, no," my dad answered. "Let me count."

"Alright," I replied. "You count," and so he did.

"One, two, three," he said in a slow and calculated voice and up he stood as I assisted him from off his bed and onto his wheelchair.

"Good job, Dad," I encouraged him as he shuffled his weight around and tried to get comfortable. Then, without warning, my mind drifted back to a time when things were a lot different.

"Ready?" I could hear my dad's voice. "One, two, three!"

"No, no," I answered, "Let me count."

"Alright," he replied, "You count," and so I did.

"One, two, three," and I jumped with all my might into the pool and into his strong arms. I'll never forget what that was like.

The memory was from a time when I was a kid and not a good swimmer. Having my dad in the pool, and knowing that he wouldn't let me drown, was just what I needed to help me overcome my fears. However, now things had changed and I was the one helping him. Funny how that happens isn't it? As my mind drifted back to my dad, now sitting in his wheelchair, I found myself overwhelmed by the love of God. It is as simple as one, two, and three.

The principle is something we never outgrow. Whether we are a child standing on the edge of a pool or we're older and struggling just to get out of bed, we all need to know that someone is there to catch us should we fall. That's what the love of God is all about.

I'm sure you would agree that this life is a bunch of never-ending challenges. For me, it feels like as soon as I overcome one thing, and begin enjoying the fruits of success, up pops a whole new challenge that I'm not quite sure that I'm ready to deal with. And so the cycle goes. "No, no," I often say to God like I used to say to my dad. "Let me count."

And, somehow, God seems willing to let me do it as long as at the end of the day I make the leap.

Though life has moved on and my dad is now in the presence of the Lord, one thing remains the same. I'm still counting to three and joyfully jumping into the strong arms of our loving heavenly Father and so can you. The same God who formed you in your mother's womb is the same God who has committed Himself to be there for you all the days of your life.

*"Hearken unto me, O house of Jacob, and all the remnant of the house of Israel, which are borne by Me from the belly, which are carried from the womb: And even to your old age I am He; and even to hoar [gray] hairs will I carry you: I have made, and I will bear; even I will carry, and will deliver you." (Isaiah 46:3-4)*

# Ebenezer Rob

The cool night air was evidence that summer was all but over. I don't know what motivated my buddies and me to wander into the graveyard that night, but I sure will never forget it. The sacred and the eerie seemed to occupy the same space.

As we wandered around, each trying to locate the oldest or most unusual gravestone, somewhere deep in my heart I knew we had no business being there.  Though as a child I had grown up near a cemetery, I don't ever recall having been in one at night. Stone after stone we went calling back and forth to each other every time we found something of interest. Being careful not to awaken any of the neighbors, or anyone else for that matter, became more and more difficult as we continued to spread apart in hopes of finding something new.

Looking back on that time in my life, it's quite clear that God was not even on my radar screen. Like most young people, I was caught up in the moment and had no real focus on things that really matter. Yet somehow, in the midst of my rebellious and wayward heart, God was getting ready to meet me right where I was.

With Bic lighter in hand and no one nearby, I stumbled upon the most shocking gravestone of the entire night. There, etched in marble, before my teenage eyes was my name:  Robert Goyette. At first glance I thought I was seeing things, but the more I looked the more I knew it was real. The initial shock was so great that I couldn't even speak or call out to my friends. God had certainly gotten my attention. Like Ebenezer Scrooge, while being shown his future, it took me a few moments for the full impact of God's message to settle in.

Who would have believed that out of all the hundreds of graves that night, I would stumble upon the one belonging to the man I was named after: my dad's uncle Rob? Though I had no idea that He was even buried there, that night it really didn't matter. The name on the stone was mine and God in His untiring pursuit of one young man had managed to catch up with me. While not aware of it at the time, I now recognize that night as a turning point in my life.

Why is it that sometimes we have to be confronted with death before we ever wake up and start thinking about life? As a young man, it's quite plain that I was clueless to the limited time we've each be given here on this earth. Psalm 90:12 says it well. "So teach us to number our days, that we might apply our hearts unto wisdom."

Though obtaining wisdom was not one of my teenage goals, I'm so glad that God took the time to get into my perishing world in order to talk to me about eternal things. Despite the fact that it took me a few years to finally get it, how wonderful it's been to be born again and tasting of eternal life.

While often frustrated by this temporal, perishing world, I've learned to place my trust in the finished work of Jesus Christ and His victory over death and the grave. What joy belongs to all those who know that their names have been written in heaven and etched in the Lambs Book of Life.

*"He that overcometh shall thus be arrayed in white garments; and I will in no wise blot his name out of the book of life, and I will confess his name before my Father, and before his angels." (Revelation 3:5)*

# Lifeboats and Knowing the Drill

Down the stairs, over the steel threshold, and out the double doors we stepped. As we did, the balmy air and ocean breeze began peeling layers of fatigue off our lives. We were on vacation. Though landing on a cruise ship was not our pick, our daughter and son-in-law had invited us. For us, being with them made it one of the most beautiful places we could possibly be.

Now I had no idea just how big a cruise ship really was, but as people streamed out the side doors and onto the lifeboat deck, I began to figure it out. There were over 3,000 passengers alone, not to mention the 1,500 staff and crew members keeping things afloat. Mind you, I didn't come up with those numbers by myself; the captain told us. In either case, the bright orange lifeboats, florescent vests worn by the crew, and mandatory participation by each passenger, made it very clear; the safety drill we were undergoing was extremely important.

Line by line, row by row, they positioned us in the very place, God forbid, we would have to abandon ship should it become necessary. It was there, in that cramped uncomfortable place, that a few interesting thoughts came to mind.

The first thing was that, when it comes to being saved, we're all on equal footing. Whether rich or poor, well-known or not, lifeboats are not segregated. From the most affluent passengers, with estate rooms and exclusive ocean views, to those just glad to be on the ship, the idea of needing to use a lifeboat leveled us all. That revelation, coupled with the thought that a provision was in place to save everyone, had me considering some weighty matters.

Though a sinking cruise ship is almost unheard of nowadays, a sinking person is not. I see it all the time. From broken families to broken individuals, people are struggling all around. Beyond that, even for those who outwardly are cruising along just fine, without accepting Jesus as savior, ultimately, we'll all perish. That, by the way is not my idea but what the Bible says very plainly. Consider this familiar verse in light of what I'm saying:

"For God so loved the world, that he gave his only begotten Son, that whosoever believeth in him should not perish, but have everlasting life. For God sent not his Son into the world to condemn the world; but that the world through him might be saved. He that believeth on him is not condemned: but he that believeth not is condemned already, because he hath not believed in the name of the only begotten Son of God." (John 3:16-18)

The good news is, unlike the Titanic, on this ship there's enough room in the lifeboats for everyone to survive. And that, according to the Scripture, is the burning desire of God's heart.

As for me and my house, we've decided to pay close attention to the instructions God has set forth for us all. Life eternal is in His Son. For those who repent and place their trust in Him, death has lost its sting and the grave its victory.

*"The Lord is not slack concerning His promise, as some men count slackness; but is longsuffering to us-ward, not willing that any should perish, but that all should come to repentance." (2 Peter 3:9)*

# Time Out To Inspect What Matters

Neither of us expected it. The sound of crackling flames threw us into a panic. With tons of bailed, shredded cardboard lying within the blazes reach, my training kicked in. By the time I managed to unzip the bright orange safety bag, and stretch out the enclosed fire hose, the fattened flames were already roaring high above the bails of paper.

I'm confident, if things had worked the way they should have, I could have squelched the fire and saved the day. Unfortunately, when my co-worker twisted open the water valve, and water went everywhere except to the nozzle I was holding, things got dramatically worse. For an instant, thoughts flashed through my mind of whose responsibility it was to have inspected that fire hose, but none of that mattered then; we were about to lose the entire place.

A wise person once said, "It's not what you expect but what you inspect that counts." That was certainly the case the day I watched tons of recycled paper go up in flames. And to think, none of it had to happen. If someone had been inspecting the fire safety equipment like they should have been, when crisis struck, we could have struck back. One thing is for sure, I'll never forget the feeling of watching huge flames grow even bigger while adequate amounts of water ran everywhere except where they needed to be.

In spiritual matters, the routine inspection of important things is equally important. The idea of just assuming that everything is ok is a bit naïve. For this cause, over and over again, the Bible encourages us to examine ourselves. Why? The answer is plain.

Without regularly inspecting our heart, its motives, and attitudes, we run the risk of being like the fire hose that failed me and my co-worker that day—full of holes and unable to fulfill our life's purpose. A good verse that comes to mind is Proverbs 4:*23* "Keep your heart with all diligence; for out of it are the issues of life." This word "issues" in the original Hebrew language literally means "boundaries." Said another way, the diligent manner by which we inspect and maintain our inner life (the heart) will determine how far we can go and how useful we can be.

When I think back on the day when fire burned and water poured in all the wrong places, it's not hard to map the analogy to so many lives I've witnessed over the years. So much potential, so much provision ("enough water to put out a forest fire") but because of neglecting to maintain the most important part, the heart, when life heats up, and it always does, things don't work the way they should.

Trust me, I'm talking about me as much as anyone. Only God officially knows how many times I've been in difficult situations and spilled water in wrong places, and I'm confident it's been more than once. Thankfully, over the years I've learned, or should I say "am learning," the importance of inspecting and maintaining my heart. By it, my life has gotten a whole lot better.

*"Search me, O God, and know my heart: try me, and know my thoughts: And see if there be any wicked way in me, and lead me in the way everlasting." (Psalm 139:23-24)*

# Bright Lights and Rearview Mirrors

Normally it wouldn't have bothered me much. For some reason on this particular day, it did. Like a one-eyed monster, the car behind me with its high beams on was obnoxious to say the least. I don't know if it was because I hadn't had my morning coffee yet, or because he was so close, but the crooked glaring light poking at my attitude through my rearview mirror was beginning to wear on me. Ironically, I was on my way to pray when it happened.

I'm not sure how it works for you, but for me, the pattern is quite predictable. It seems like distractions and annoying things always appear at times when I'm heading toward life's important stuff. On this particular day, it certainly was the case. When the thought finally occurred to me to reach up and flip my rearview mirror so that the light was no longer shining directly in my eyes, I had no idea how God was getting ready to speak to me. The relief I experienced as the glaring light took a back seat made God's words all the more powerful.

"I want you to learn how to do that in other areas of your life as well," He said matter-of-factly. The "that" He was referring to was clear. The little flip of the mirror was the lesson He wanted me to learn. Once I considered how that practice translated to the other areas of my life, a wonderful freedom began flooding my soul.

Now those of you who have ever had a car pull up behind you with their high beams on and have known to flip that little tab on the review mirror, you know just what I'm talking about. Somehow, you can still see the vehicle behind you, but its glaring lights are no longer in your face. It's really a neat invention. The fact that the same principle works in other areas of our lives is even more amazing. When we don't utilize such a wonderful provision, we often end up letting other things dictate the attitude with which we are driving—I'm talking spiritually of course.

I once heard it said that fifty percent of all leadership is knowing what to ignore. I have to agree. Though learning to flip the mirror on life's annoying things is not the same as completely ignoring them, the basic result is still the same. When I learn to flip my God given mirror,

I'm free to move forward without being overly distracted from my vision and mission in life.

I have to tell you, on the day God spoke this truth to me, my time of prayer went to a whole new level. From one situation to the next, I found myself flipping mirrors and getting my eyes back where they belonged. As a side note, when we employ this truth, the subtle irritations that often barge into our lives find themselves in the back seat where they belong. All that said, I'm just glad that I don't have to live at the mercy of every bright light that tends to pull me backwards and not forward.

*"Brethren, I count not myself to have apprehended: but this one thing I do, forgetting those things which are behind, and reaching forth unto those things which are before, I press toward the mark for the prize of the high calling of God in Christ Jesus." (Philippians 3:13-14)*

# Wooden Giraffes and Dangling Arms

Her yell surprised us all. If I hadn't been there, I might not have believed it. The sight of her frail dangling arm, hanging from the window, is one I won't soon forget. And to think, the guy responsible for it was me. Worse yet, the African pastor who was hosting us caught the whole thing on film.

We were in Kenya, East Africa and I was running on fumes. With long days of preaching and teaching just behind us, and little to no sleep hanging on me like a lead vest at the dentist office. I was ready to be back home.

When the elderly woman approached our car trying to sell us more wooden giraffes, my outward demeanor was pleasant and pastoral. By the time she forced a giraffe into my hands and then let it go and began demanding money, inwardly, things began to change. Though she was quite rude, by God's grace I managed to keep my cool. "Thank you, ma'am," I told her. "I've already bought some."

"Two dolla," she said, assuming a good deal would change my mind.

"No thank you," I said again. "I have no room to carry it back home."

"Ok, ok," she said more insistently. "Tree dolla," and with that pushed the giraffe back at me as I tried to give it to her. It was that statement that brought both a chuckle and the lens cap off my host pastor's video camera.

When I finally got the giraffe back into her hands, and began to close the window, I had forgotten about the problems we had been having with the window. For some reason, sometimes it worked and sometimes it didn't. This time, as I flipped the switch to close it, it wouldn't stop. I know—terrible right? Trust me, I felt horrible. Be assured, I did everything I could to get the window back down and the poor lady's arm out as quickly as I could. Needless to say, she didn't try to sell me any more giraffes but if she had, I would have bought ten in an attempt to free myself from the unintended guilt I was experiencing.

The sticking power of guilt and shame never cease to amaze me. Even for things that we had no intention of doing, guilt and shame are like magnets drawn to the sin nature into which we were all born. As someone who has spent his fair share of time in the ring wrestling through those issues, I by no means consider myself a novice in the arena of learning how to live with a conscience void of offense.

Though being able to tell ourselves "I didn't mean to do that," does ease some of the sting, it never ultimately deals with the problem. The reason—at the root of all guilt and shame is our need for a Savior. No matter how hard I may strive in my own goodness to be good, I always come up short. That, by the way, is something we either believe or we prove; it is what it is. The good news is, that in the places we come up short, Jesus has triumphed on our behalf. As we place our faith and trust in Him, His payment and victory over sin, and ultimately guilt and shame, is imparted to us.

*"There is therefore now no condemnation to them which are in Christ Jesus, who walk not after the flesh, but after the Spirit." (Romans 8:1)*

# Giving What You've Received

There they were again. As usual, they always showed up at the most inopportune of times. I suppose the fact that it was in my mind that they showed up, was more my issue than theirs, but in either case, making them leave seemed impossible.

The truth is, I was having a difficult time forgiving someone. I know as a pastor you're supposed to have it all together, but let me just be real with you. I was struggling. Though it was many years ago, the feeling of being stuck in un-forgiveness was one of the most horrible feelings I've ever had. It seemed that every time I would try to forget the past and move on, somehow, there in my mind, that person would appear—without invitation—often invading holy moments of prayer and communion with God.

I'll never forget the day that God sat me down and gave me one of those Father-son talks. Evidently, my problem was not so much the deepness of the wound I had received, but that I was trying to fabricate forgiveness on my own, as if forgiveness originated in me. How awesome it was to realize that real forgiveness always begins with God!

God's words to me that day went something like this: "If someone asks you for $10 and you don't have it, it's totally okay to tell them you don't have it; in essence, you can't give what you don't have. If, on the other hand, I give you $10 and then someone ask you for $10, it's a lie if you tell them you don't have it. All I'm asking you to do Rob is to give to them what I've given to you."

Though in principle I had known that for years, that day God's words to me clicked. From then on, every time that particular person showed up in my mind waiving the offense, instead of straining to produce forgiveness for them on my own, I simply remembered all the times God had forgiven me. It was amazing to see how rich in forgiveness I really was. Once I began to give the person that which God had given me, the offense left and I was free.

Interesting, isn't it? For years, I had walked in a measure of forgiveness toward others, but never before had I been so deeply challenged. For the longest time I had thought I understood how forgiveness worked, but now, through a horrible set of circumstances, I had experienced forgiveness at a completely new level. For that, I am eternally grateful.

As is always the case, things that produce real and lasting results always have their origin in God Himself. When it comes to forgiveness, no one knows how it works better than Jesus. Here are His words: "For if you forgive men their trespasses, your heavenly Father will also forgive you: But if you forgive not men their trespasses, neither will your Father forgive your trespasses." (Matthew 6:14-15)

This straightforward verse only confirms what I experienced that day. My ability to forgive others was directly related to the forgiveness I had received. I, like most of you, have had plenty of opportunities to get offended and to hold people in un-forgiveness. In like fashion, I, like most of you, have received a ton of God's forgiveness. After taking an inventory of my account with God, I have decided to freely give as I have freely received. In this way, God's grace keeps flowing both to me and through me. The end result has been extremely liberating.

*"And as you go, preach, saying, The kingdom of heaven is at hand. Heal the sick, raise the dead, cleanse the lepers, cast out demons: freely you received, freely give." (Matthew 10:7-8)*

# Be Careful What You Carry Around

When she finally looked down and realized what she was holding, she was horrified. And to think, the whole time she had been strutting down the aisle like Miss America she thought people were staring at her because of her good looks.

It all began while visiting the bathroom on the train. Though I wasn't there, to hear my friend tell the story is quite funny. The woman evidently had spent a little too much time in front of the mirror gazing at herself. When she left the bathroom, she grabbed what she thought was her purse and tucked it up under arm. It wasn't until she made it all the way back to her seat that she realized what she had done.

There, up under her arm, instead of her fashionable clutch purse, was a fresh roll of toilet paper that had been sitting on the counter. Somehow, in her pre-occupation with herself, she had not looked down to see what she was grabbing. When it finally hit her, the embarrassment was quite a blow. Especially when she had to walk all the way back down the aisle to retrieve her purse.

Self-absorption is an interesting thing. The more of it we have, the blinder we become to what's happening around us. I find the principle true in a variety of different settings. Whether we are talking about our own personal lives, the church we attend, or the country we live in, if we spend too much time pondering our own perceived greatness, we tend to lose perspective on what's really going on around us. The result is typically not pretty.

All I'm doing is offering an observation and, unfortunately, a confession of my own failure in this area. I can't even begin to tell you how many times over the years I've carried things around that weren't even mine, and all because I was too self-focused. Fortunately, when reality finally hits, and it always does, the pain of it is not soon forgotten.

Perhaps you're asking if it's wrong to look at yourself in the mirror, or to think that your church is the greatest church on the planet, or to be proud to be an American? Absolutely not! The problem, however, occurs when we think that we are the center of the universe instead of God, Who has given us everything that we have. Anytime we lose sight of Him, we, like the woman who was strutting down the aisle, are getting ready to discover our true condition.

As for me, I try to pay close attention to the things I pick up. Though the cross is not the most convenient thing to carry around, its benefits and rewards remain unsurpassed by any of life's experiences.

Jesus' advice to us on this matter is extremely challenging, but powerful to all who dare to embrace it:

*"Then said Jesus unto his disciples, If any man will come after me, let him deny himself, and take up his cross, and follow me. For whosoever will save his life shall lose it: and whosoever will lose his life for my sake shall find it." (Matthew 16:24-25)*

# Little Things That Really Matter

The room burst into flames. Though most of us were asleep when it happened, my two friends were right in the middle of it. If it hadn't been for their cries for help, I'm sure we would have just kept on sleeping.

It all happened over 30 years ago while I was serving on a peer ministry team in northern Vermont. Our mission was simple: to host a weekend youth retreat for the church that I was attending. The building that we had rented, old and a bit historic, seemed the perfect place to hold the annual event. That was until the kitchen burst into flames of course. As you might imagine, the explosion that earned both my friends an ambulance ride was not on our list of spiritual events planned for the weekend. That said, it sure did grab everyone's attention. And to think, it all happened because of something so small.

Now if you know anything about gas stoves, you know about the pilot light. It's that little flame that stays burning all the time, waiting for someone to turn on the gas. Nowadays, if the pilot light goes out, it automatically shuts off the supply valve so that you don't run the risk of filling the room with gas. That, by the way, is what happened to my friends. Somehow, the gas from the antique stove had been running all night long and had filled every nook of the old kitchen. By the time my friends got up to start making breakfast, the room was a bomb waiting to go off. Thankfully, they both survived.

It never ceases to amaze me how little things can create such big problems. Whether we are talking about little flames that have gone out, gas valves that are left running, or, more importantly, unresolved relationship issues with one another, it's pretty much all the same. If we don't fix things quickly, one day it's sure to blow up, and as a result, people will suffer.

The Song of Solomon 2:15a has this to say, "Take us the foxes, the little foxes that spoil the vines…"

My experience has been that it is usually the little things that end up spoiling the wonderful plans God has for our lives. You might not agree, but I challenge you to look back over your life and to consider any situation that turned into a big mess. I think you have to admit, with almost no exception, all big problems start as little things that simply grow out of control. Like it or not, if we don't pay attention to the small stuff, it will become the big stuff real quick.

That being the case, perhaps the most powerful small thing on the planet is our tongue. The apostle James puts it pretty bluntly: "Behold, we put bits in the horses' mouths, that they may obey us; and we turn about their whole body. Behold also the ships, which though they be so great, and are driven of fierce winds, yet are they turned about with a very small helm, whithersoever the governor listeth. Even so the tongue is a little member, and boasteth great things. Behold, how great a matter a little fire kindleth!" (James 3:3-5)

Nowadays I'm increasingly aware of my need for God's help when it comes to the power of my tongue. Though at times our words seem like little things, the truth is, if they go unpoliced, they can sure end up hurting others.

*"For every kind of beasts, and of birds, and of serpents, and of things in the sea, is tamed, and hath been tamed of mankind: But the tongue can no man tame; it is an unruly evil, full of deadly poison."*
*(James 3:7-8)*

# Barstool Preacher

As I preached, they listened. The only problem was, I wasn't walking with the Lord and neither were they. Looking back, I hate to think about the confusing content of my message. Strangely, I know God was working with me even there. Oh yeah, I forgot to tell you where I was. I was in a bar in Burlington, Vermont and my so-called "congregation" was sitting on bar stools as clueless about God as I was. All I knew at the time was that there was something more to life and I was determined to find it. So, I preached what I thought it was all about and they listened.

It may seem hard to believe, but I'm convinced that even back then God was preparing me for what I'm doing today. I find that idea fascinating. When I look at my past, I can't deny God's sovereign hand guiding me toward His intended purpose for my life. Actually, I believe it works that way for all of us. Though God never forces His will on anyone, He's constantly working with us in the hope that we'll see the benefit of doing things His way.

God told Jeremiah, "Before I formed you in the belly I knew you; and before you came forth out of the womb I sanctified you, and I ordained you a prophet unto the nations." (Jeremiah 1:5)

Have you ever considered the idea that God made you with something specific in mind? Have you ever considered the idea that it is there, in the center of God's will, that you will be the most satisfied? I know I have. Truth is I've tried both options: living to what I think is right for my life and living to the will of God. Hands down, living to the will of God is best.

For me, not to understand the beauty of divine design is like using a riding lawnmower to drive back and forth to work. Sure, it's doable, but it's not the way it's supposed to be. Like trying to eat Jell-O with chopsticks, living outside God's intended purpose for your life is sure to leave you frustrated and hungry.

I know that not everyone is supposed to be a pastor like me, but that doesn't negate the point. Each of us was born with something beautiful and specific in mind. Understanding that, and then pursuing that, is what this life is all about. Thankfully, God stands ever ready to help us figure it all out.

I have to tell you, when I finally surrendered to His constant prodding and exchanged my will for His, it was amazing how all the pieces came together. I can honestly say, though I've had many challenges, I'm happier today than I've ever been, and I know it's because I'm doing the thing God intended for my life.

While I no longer preach in bars, though I've had the thought and remain open to the idea, I do look for every opportunity to share the Good News. The news that says every life counts and has a purpose. News that says God values that purpose so much that He was willing to pay the ultimate price, the life of His son on the cross. News that says we are forgiven, and now, by His grace, have an opportunity to start our lives afresh, this time in the center of His will. To me it doesn't get any better than that.

*"Delight yourself also in the Lord; and He shall give you the desires of your heart. Commit you way unto the Lord; trust also in Him; and He shall bring it to pass." (Psalm 37:4-5)*

# Kisses, Relays And Running For God

I'll never forget my first kiss. Actually, the girl kissed *me*. I just sat there in shock. Besides kisses from my mom and older sisters, being kissed by a girl was as foreign and awkward of a thing that this first grader could have ever experienced.

Geri was her name, and I have to tell you she was kind of cute. Apparently, she thought the same thing about me. The only problem was, I didn't see it coming.

With my eyes focused on the relay race our gym class was doing, and trying to sit cross-legged and single file just like Mrs. Casey had told us to, Geri's sizzling kiss struck me like a hot branding iron. From just behind me in the line, she literally pulled me over backwards, kissed me on the forehead, and then let me go. I'm not sure, but I think it was the first time I ever blushed.

Thankfully, the whole thing took place just moments before it was my turn to run in the relay race and *oh,* how I *ran!* Now in case you're wondering, I wasn't running fast in attempt to get away from what had happened, but because of what had happened.

The idea that Geri, one of the cutest girls in my first-grade class, liked me was enough to make me run like Eric Liddell in the 1981 Oscar winning film "Chariots of Fire." If you've not seen the movie, I highly recommend it. It's a classic. In either case, running because of love, to me, is what life is all about.

While it's true that I was just in the first grade, it's also true that way down in the fiber of every human being is a desire to receive and to give love. I'm not talking about sensual lust; I'm talking about Love. Though people and evil things have perverted and abused it, true love is the reason we all exist.

Now that brings us to an interesting point. According to the Bible, God is love (1 John.4:8). So, we could say it like this: if the dominant need of the human heart is love, and God is love, then the dominant need of the human heart is really God. The problem seems to be in the way that we see Him. Often viewed as an angry old man sitting on His throne, waiting to throw lightning bolts at us every time we make a mistake, is it any wonder people run from God instead of for Him? I know for the longest time that's the way it was for me. Until the day He snuck up behind me that is.

Like the fishermen, tax collectors, prostitutes and others contained in the Gospels, when I finally realized Who it was that was pursuing me, my whole life changed. Though I'm keenly aware that my part in this relay race is a small one, the kiss that heaven gave to earth some 2000 years ago is what has me running hard today.

*"In this was manifested the love of God toward us, because that God sent His only begotten Son into the world, that we might live through Him. Herein is love, not that we loved God but that He loved us, and sent His Son to be the propitiation for our sins." (1 John 4:9-10)*

*"Let Him kiss me with the kisses of His mouth: for your love is better than wine." (Song of Solomon 1:2)*

# Life, Death, and Surprise Reunions

The cool breeze swirled behind her as she closed the door. Finally, back inside. It had been a hard winter, especially because she hadn't heard from her son. The hope that he would be home for Christmas had come and gone. Now, just believing he was still alive was all she had to cling to.

The year was 1945 and my father-in-law was one of thousands of U.S. Marines coming home from World War 2. For them, the logistical chaos surrounding their return was a walk in the park compared to all that they had been through. For my father-in-law, Fernando Floyd, anywhere besides Guadalcanal was a welcome place to be.

Though he hit Seattle, Washington wearing only a summer uniform in the dead of winter, to be on U.S. soil was a dream come true. By the time he found himself swinging open the gate that led to his house, the distant sounds of war still ringing in his head, suddenly ceased. For his mother, who had no idea he was back in the States, his unannounced return had an even greater impact. It had been five years since she had seen him.

I don't know about you, but I love true stories, especially when they involve struggles, faith, and triumphant endings. The story of my father-in-law pushing open the front door and saying "Mom, I'm home!" is certainly one of my favorites. You can only imagine how it hit her. When he finally rounded the corner into the kitchen where she was, she literally fainted. God had answered her travailing prayers. You can be sure, when she woke, Laredo, Texas was never the same.

Many years have passed since that day, and so has my father-in-law. But the story doesn't end there. According to the Bible (1 Thess 4:13-18), he, along with all those who have died in the Lord, will return one more time. Oh, what a day that will be! For those who've lost loved ones because of death, the Bible offers great hope and comfort. Like Fernando Floyd who surprised his mother that day, for all who put their trust in Jesus, a glorious reunion is just around the corner.

www.ingramcontent.com/pod-product-compliance
Lightning Source LLC
Chambersburg PA
CBHW080606090426
42735CB00017B/3356